W0006840

The *Miseducation* *of the* Christian

The Miseducation *of the* Christian

Dr. Valerie K. Brown

CREATION
HOUSE
A STRANG COMPANY

The Miseducation of the Christian
by Dr. Valerie K. Brown
Published by Creation House
A Strang Company
600 Rinehart Road
Lake Mary, Florida 32746
www.creationhouse.com

Unless otherwise noted, all Scripture quotations are from
the Holy Bible, New Living Translation, copyright © 1996.
Used by permission of Tyndale House Publishers, Inc.,
Wheaton, IL 60189. All rights reserved.

Scripture quotations marked KJV are from the
King James Version of the Bible.

Cover design by Terry Clifton

Library of Congress Control Number: 2007920196
International Standard Book Number: 978-1-59979-168-5

First Edition

07 08 09 10 11 — 987654321
Printed in the United States of America

Contents

Foreword vi

Preface x

Introduction. xvi

1   Myths Surrounding Jesus and Money 1

2   God's Original Plan for Our Financial Freedom 19

3   Managing Our Money God's Way 41

4   Getting Your Financial House in Order 69

Conclusion 88

Appendix: Biblical Financial Spending
    Plan and Worksheet 92

Epilogue. 99

Notes 100

About the Author 101

Foreword

New believers in Christ today are different from Christians a generation ago. When I became a Christian—a long time ago, longer than I care to remember—we simply went to church, listened to the pastor and our various Sunday school teachers, and believed what they told us about what the Bible says. We were what I call "passive learners." As I have come to a deeper understanding of what it means to be a Christian, I have obtained a better understanding of God and the Bible by asking more questions rather than being a passive learner. This seems to be the paradigm for most believers of Christ today. We are not content with traditional ways and values of doing church. Nor are we content with answers given extemporaneously from church leaders with no biblical support. We want to see and understand God's wisdom as it is found in the Bible. Our discontent with the status quo and our zeal to fully understand the Bible have led active-learner Christians of today to challenge church leaders. We want our pastors to show us the biblical support for the answers they give by quoting book, chapter, and verse, so that we can study the lessons ourselves and learn why as Christians we do certain things but do not do other things.

Astonishingly enough, many of the things we have held as sacred in the church cannot be justified biblically. They can, however, be justified through traditional ways of operating or denominational doctrine. More and more, active learners are finding that the things we do in church are not in the Word of God. We have been doing things or saying things because they are what we were taught, or are what our denomination says we should do if we are to adhere properly to our particular denomination's doctrine.

As with all my writings, this book is not to criticize any previous teachings or denominational traditions. I seek to provide biblical support to timely and profound topics that have been creating quite a controversy among church leadership and laity. The answers as found in the Word of God surrounding these topics will unravel or shake many of the beliefs we have held to be true for so many years. If we could truly study, understand, and believe the Word of God as it relates to these topics, we would be holding the "keys of the Kingdom" right here on earth (Matt. 16:19).

What are the topics? Money and theology. Christians today want to know how to connect their spiritual theology toward money to their practical theology. For purposes of this book, we are defining the term spiritual theology as our understanding of what the Bible has to say about money; our understanding of God's plan for our financial stewardship (Old Testament); and our understanding of Jesus and His thoughts about wealth and possessions, relating to our effort to be like Jesus (New Testament). Our practical theology can be described as what we should actually be doing everyday with our finances: should we be paying tithes? Giving offerings? Paying our bills in a timely manner? Simply put, how can we take what the Word of God says about money and apply it to our everyday life?

My daughter came home from a youth Bible study one evening and told me that she had learned that the letters of the word Bible stood for:

B—Biblical

I—Instructions

B—Before

L—Leaving

E—Earth

If we look at it that way—that Bible stands for Biblical Instructions Before Leaving Earth—it would follow that we must read the Bible daily to know what it says about how we should be living. It is amazing how many Christians have not read the Bible from beginning to end. It is even more amazing that Christians do not go to the Word of God for answers to their everyday problems. This leads us to the first question: do we *really* believe the Word of God has the answers to our daily problems? Or, do we believe the Bible is merely a good story? Actions displayed by most Christians indicate that somewhere, somehow, they have been taught that the Word of God is something you read on Sunday, but then put away until Wednesday night Bible Study or the following Sunday morning. Living that way, it is no wonder we still have unanswered questions to simple problems.

I invite you to follow along as I attempt to answer several questions frequently asked of church leaders on the topics of money and theology. We will go to the Word of God for our guidance. My prayer before we begin addressing these topics is that God will inspire the words that follow so that flesh and blood will not be answering these questions, but God Himself as He anoints our pursuit of His wisdom. Amen.

Preface

The topics of money and theology are perhaps the most difficult to talk about and gather consensus about what the Word of God teaches. What we can agree upon, however, is that the Bible spends a great deal of time, either through scriptures or parables taught by Jesus, addressing the topic of money and what our attitude toward money ought to be. The *New Believer's Bible* says the following under the topic of giving to God in its First Steps:

> Money is such an important topic in the Bible that it is the main subject of nearly half the parables Jesus told. In addition, one out of every seven verses in the New Testament deals with the topic. To give you an idea of how this compares with other topics, Scripture offers about five hundred verses on prayer and fewer than five hundred on faith, while there are more than two thousand verses on money![1]

Since so much of the Bible is devoted to the topic of money, we can reasonably conclude that money would be a difficult burden for the Christian to overcome. Can you imagine? If more preachers were like

Jesus, every other Sunday they would preach about money. If preachers tried to balance their sermon subjects based on the percentages of Bible versus, then a preacher would preach one Sunday on faith, three Sundays on money; one Sunday on prayer, and three Sundays on money—I think we get the message! If preachers did this, they would be run out of the pulpits. Yet, a preacher can preach four Sundays straight on faith or love or mercy or grace, any of the good news text, and not one member will say, "When is Pastor going to stop preaching on (fill in the blank)?" Yet if a pastor preachers two Sundays in a row on money, half the congregation will think to themselves, *Is that all he can talk about?*

Why is it that we never tire of hearing about love, faith, grace, mercy, and forgiveness from the pulpit? All of these topics are supported by the Bible, so why is it that if the preacher quotes book, chapter, and verse about money, we shudder until the sermon is over? Can it be we need to renew our minds about money and theology?

It is apparent from our actions and conversations that we do not like to talk about money, therefore it is not a surprise that so many Christians are in debt or struggling through some kind of financial crisis. It is our inability to talk openly about money that reveals why so many Christians are flocking to the prosperity preachers who teach how to get out of debt and receive God's blessings in the area of finances. Christians are looking for someone within the Christian community who will address money and theology using the Bible as the source, rather than tradition, biased opinions, and ignorance about what the Bible really says.

It is unfortunate, however, that many prosperity preachers have been labeled as evil or money hungry. The amazing revelation for me, however, is that church members never label the forgiveness preachers—preachers who only preach about love, salvation, grace, or any of the good news topics in the Bible—as evil.

> **Christians will always find "bad apples" among those preaching the gospel, whether they preach about money or the love of Christ. We simply cannot use them to justify throwing out the entire barrel.**

Why is that? It is because the topic of money is so personal to us. Society establishes, unfortunately, our value as individuals based on our net worth. Many of us pretend to be more than we are. We live beyond our means and are afraid to let anyone know. We are living paycheck to paycheck—the first time any crisis comes along, we can find ourselves one step from filing for bankruptcy.

Instead of talking negatively about the prosperity preachers, we should be going to the Bible and determining if what they are teaching can be found there. If what they are teaching is in the Word of God, then who are we to have a problem with the message? They are simply the messengers. And perhaps that is the answer—as in biblical times, a messenger quite often was killed because of the message they delivered. (See 2 Samuel 4:9–10.) The burden becomes ours whether we want to apply the principles in our lives. If we cannot find what they are teaching in the Word of God, then the Word is clear that we should flee quickly from false teachers. (See Romans 16:17; 1 John 4.)

As Christians, we should be striving for a balanced life in Christ. A balanced Christian life is more than learning about the Word of God as it applies to financial blessings. A balanced Christian life is studying the entire Bible. I am a strong supporter of prosperity teachings because I believe in the entire Word of God and I have found scriptures and parables to support prosperity teachings. I am also a strong supporter of prosperity teachings because finance is an area that has been neglected for a long time, due to the backlash that preachers must face when teaching those principles. Let me also say at this point, that there are always bad apples in the barrel who manipulate the Bible for their own personal gain. I am not including them in this dialogue on those who teach practical or prosperity living. However, we cannot become strong, mature Christians if we do not have balanced teachings.

The Word of God uses the body many times as symbolism for Christ. (See Ephesians 4; 1 Corinthians 12:12.) In everyday life, when we see strong, healthy bodies, we know that the owner of the body has provided a balanced program of food, nutrition, and exercise in order to perfect the body. Your spiritual growth and maturity are no different. You must balance your knowledge in Christ with as much financial knowledge as you also have about love, salvation, grace, and mercy. A body with only one strong, well-developed muscle cannot operate as well as a body that has had all of its muscles developed.

I say all of this simply to take the opportunity, before we begin our discussion of the miseducation of the Christian, to state that I am not one-dimensional. However, as 1 Timothy 6:10 tells us, the *love* of money is the root of evil. Therefore most of the ills of our society can be traced back to money: the lack of it, the greed for it, and the mismanagement of it. However, never can we trace societal ills back to money simply because one possesses it. It is not the money that is the problem—it is society and its warped perception of it.

We all know there is more to God's Word than financial blessing. However, there is a pressing need for Christians to tackle the subjects of money and theology. This book is the opportunity to open that dialogue and, once and for all, find answers to questions about money and the Bible.

Introduction

There is a common sentiment among Christians whenever we try to address the relationship between money and doctrine that "Jesus was financially poor, and since we are striving to be like Jesus in everyway, we should also be poor." It is this sentiment that constantly accompanies the question, "Can Christians be financially wealthy and remain holy, Christlike, and go to heaven?" Is it true that everyone who has obtained wealth did so through unscrupulous or ungodly ways, motives, or methods? These are just a sample of the varied questions concerning money and theology that have been raised over the generations. If you ask most Christians whether or not Jesus was financially poor while here on earth, and if that was His desire for us, they likely would respond with, "Yes, I believe Jesus was financially poor." Then, when you follow up on that answer with, "Can you tell me how you know that Jesus was financially poor? Did you read it in the Bible? Did you hear a pastor say that? Did you read it somewhere other than the Bible?" you will normally get responses such as:

I do not know—it's just what I believe.

Yes, I heard a pastor say that.

Yes, I read it in a biblically based textbook… but not the Bible itself.

Can't really say, but I know I was taught that in Sunday school, coming up in the church as a little child.

Every Christmas the church produces a play depicting the birth of Jesus as born to poor parents in a barn, because they could not afford a room in the inn.

Every Easter (Resurrection Sunday) the media (television, Broadway) produces a story on the life of Jesus and He is portrayed as having been a homeless, barefoot beggar.

Too many myths, intentional or unintentional comments, visual productions, and opinions, rather than what the Bible actually says, are the main reasons Christians do not have a healthy understanding of money and theology. We, as leaders of the Christian faith, have done our members a great disservice in our teaching (or lack thereof) on money and the Bible. As bad parents sometimes do with their children, we have allowed everyone—those not in the church, the world, and the media—to tell us how we should think and respond to any conversations about money and theology. We believe those two words do not belong in the same sentence. Nor should we talk about whether we believe Jesus was financially rich or poor. How can we not have that conversation when the premise of our everyday Christian lifestyle is predicated on who Jesus was or was not?

Most Christians will agree that we are trying to be like Jesus. We believe that Jesus is the Example we should follow in our everyday living. If that is what we truly believe, then we must take the time to explore who Jesus was, and learn how the nature of His character should influence our attitude toward money.

We in America, as well as some foreign countries, live in a society where individuals are experiencing unprecedented personal financial gains. This explosion in personal wealth has caused the financially successful Christian to raise questions previously articulated. Are they now sinful because they have achieved what they were taught was unholy? Do they have to give away all of their hard earned finances in order to go to heaven?

Many churches across America are home to middle class families. While their struggle may not be homelessness, hunger, poverty, or any of the other trials associated with the lack of financial resources, their struggle to understand salvation and to be saved, within the context of their affluence, remains an important need that they desire to be addressed. Few will argue that the primary purpose of the church is the universal commission to save souls by making disciples who then go out and make other disciples. The Bible does not distinguish in that commission between saving poor or rich souls—the Bible means *all* souls.

It is not surprising, therefore, that some church leaders are rising to the occasion to teach on personal financial wealth and its biblical meaning. This new prosperity teaching can be compared to the early settlers exploring the new frontier. Early settlers were challenged to move away from the safety and comfort of established territory to go out and find new land. This new frontier promised many things and many went for different reasons. It promised a challenge, a struggle, harsh conditions; yet it also promised financial riches through land acquisition, gold to be discovered, new leadership opportunities, and increased flocks and herds, to name but a few. Those who dared to be the first to go were often ridiculed by those who desired the comfort and safety of established territory. Yet, something tugged constantly at the souls of those who were called to conquer the wild West. They could not stay long in one place, for they knew there was more to this newfound land than where they were. Some were very successful, while others lost their lives.

Teaching on prosperity has proven to be no different. The church has gone through its history of frontier stories. Those who have been in the church for at least thirty years know the history. The church had its season of fire and brimstone preachers. There was a time when preachers only preached sin and death with hell as everyone's final destination. Church members were so beat-up, cut-up, and bloody, that many left the church because perfection in their lifestyle was simply not attainable. Then the new preachers on the block started teaching grace and mercy. Many of the fire and brimstone pastors talked negatively about these new preachers teaching all this love stuff. However, for those of us able to look back, we have the benefit of seeing that the next frontier was simply coming into being and what was considered heresy at that time—all that grace, love, and forgiveness—was truly biblical and needed to be taught to the Christian community.

Now, the settlers are restless once again, realizing there is more to this salvation message than simply going to heaven. The new frontier beckons with the question, "How about life right here on earth? What kind of lifestyle should a Christian enjoy? What type of lifestyle should a Christian be exemplifying? What does it really mean to 'be like Jesus?'" Thus, we have entered the next frontier of practical life teaching and preaching. The mission of this practical life teaching and preaching is to provide an understanding for the Christian of how to use and incorporate their theological understanding of the Bible into their everyday life. It is the practical teaching and preaching that is beginning to show the Christian that what they do and say on Sunday is not different from what they say and do once they leave the confines of their church building. It is this practical teaching and preaching that admonishes the Christian to walk their faith through their actions and lifestyles Monday through Saturday and not just on Sunday in church. Yes, this practical teaching and preaching is glad to know that you are going to be saved and go to heaven (in the by and by); yet this teaching and preaching is more joyous to know that you are experiencing the love, joy, peace and prosperity of heaven right here on earth as it is in heaven. Therefore, it is this teaching and preaching that speaks to our finances, our marriages, our families, our entire lifestyle and compares it to the Bible to see if God would be pleased with what we are doing with all that He has entrusted with us as his stewards.

Christians have explored and conquered the territories of fire and brimstone—knowing what is sinful and what is not, whether we want to acknowledge it or live that way—and love, grace, and mercy.

We know Jesus paid the ultimate price and was the Sacrifice for our sins so that we can be forgiven and go to heaven. This is about how to get saved, receive salvation, and go to heaven. Now Christians want to know how to get what Christ taught when He taught us how to pray in Matthew 6:9–13 (KJV), "Thy kingdom come…on earth as it is in heaven."

This new cadre of frontier preachers teaching practical life applications, including prosperity teaching, has their critics. Are we surprised? We shouldn't be. History does repeat itself and this is no different. At this point in history, however, we do not have the benefit of hindsight that the next generation will have. As with all gospel teaching and preaching, our focus should be on the biblical support used for whatever is taught. Does the message come directly from the Word of God? Did the teacher identify the book, chapter, and verse so that we can have the opportunity to go and read it for ourselves? If the message is so biblically grounded, who are we to question the messenger?

CHAPTER 1

Myths Surrounding Jesus and Money

I f a definitive Yes or No answer is given to the "Was Jesus rich or poor?" question, we would be deciding the fate of the reader for the rest of this book. If the answer is Yes, Jesus was financially rich while here on Earth, then those who believe He (Jesus) was financially poor would simply close the book right here and not read any further. If the answer is no—and Jesus was financially poor—Christians who have obtained wealth would be dealt a devastating blow and left to ponder how and why God would allow them to obtain such wealth and riches, if not in His plan for their lives. So, rather than answer yes or no, let's see what the Bible has to say on the subject and let us each draw our own conclusions as to what the Bible says rather than what man has taught us. Since we are also discussing myths—images that have depicted Christ as a poor person, and misconceptions of Christ—we will also take this opportunity to discuss those as well.

Misconception #1: The Birth of Jesus

There is no better place to start than the birth of Jesus. No other story, perhaps other than the Resurrection of Jesus, is told, either verbally or through drama, more frequently. If one asked a Christian if this story depicted Jesus or his family, Mary and Joseph, as either financially poor or rich, most would immediately say they were poor because Joseph could not afford to pay for a room at the inn when Mary was due for delivery. Baby Jesus had to be born in a manger; his parents could not do any better financially. This is how the story is normally told or visually depicted. But if one would read the story as told in the Gospel of Luke 2:6–7 we would find these words:

> And while they were there, the time came for her baby to be born. She gave birth to her first child, a son. She wrapped him snugly in strips of cloth and laid him in a manger, because there was no room for them in the village inn.

We all know this passage well. The Roman Emperor Augustus had decreed that a census be taken of all the citizens. All the citizens, therefore, had to travel to their hometown to be counted and registered in the census. Naturally, Joseph took Mary with him to Bethlehem, his hometown, to be registered. Joseph had to travel from Nazareth in Galilee to Bethlehem in Judea. We must remember the times and recognize that Joseph and Mary had to travel by horse, mule, or camel for that was the common mode of transportation. It was a slow journey, although thousands had to do the same, as it had been decreed by the emperor. The scripture does not say how long it took for Mary and Joseph to travel from one location to the next; but we can safely assume that the journey was far enough that Joseph was not going to be able to go back home that same night. One can safely assume that since the scripture speaks to his need for lodging that night. How and why would the scripture reference the fact, however, that there was no room in the inn if Joseph did not at least inquire as to whether or not there were any rooms left? Keep in mind there were no credit cards or phones to call ahead and reserve a room. During those days, it was first come, first served for the rooms. Let us also not forget that a convention was in town—the census—and most had traveled quite some distance and needed a place to stay. The point here is how many people go and inquire for a room if they had no way of paying for the room? We will exclude at this point, for argument's sake, those who are divinely connected with Jesus and go in on faith to inquire about a room. The reality is that not many of us do that. Therefore, this first myth or false depiction that Jesus was born in a manger because His family could not afford a room simply does not line up with the text. Joseph must have had at least enough money at that point to pay for a room had a room been available.

The traditional Christmas story, or birth of Christ, usually does not end there. There are always the wise men at the birth of Jesus. If you ask a Christian, how many wise men were there, most will answer that there were three. Ask them how they know there were three wise men and once again, most will say because that is what they have heard or seen depicted. The text in Matthew 2:7–12 tells the story of the wise men. The scripture never tells us how many wise men there were, nor does the scripture say the wise men were present at the birth. We naturally assume there were three wise men because we know that they brought three types gifts to Mary and Joseph in celebration of the birth of Jesus: gold, frankincense, and myrrh. For all we know, there could have been twenty wise men all bearing these gifts or there could have been as few as two wise men simply using camels to carry their treasure chests. The point to raising this scriptural reference is twofold: one, the wise men were not there when Jesus was born and lying in the manger; and two, they brought expensive gifts. The first point again gives credibility to the argument that Christians rely too heavily on what others tell them or what they see dramatized than in reading the Word of God on their own and finding out what it says. This passage in Matthew clearly states that it had been over two years since the birth of Jesus by the time they got to see Him (see Matthew 2:16); yet Christians will argue, argue, argue, that the wise men were indeed present at the birth. Secondly, we cannot overlook the expensive gifts since we are discussing whether Jesus was financially rich or not. We might not be able to put a price tag on the value of the frankincense and myrrh; but we certainly know the value of gold. The text does not say how many chests of gold there were, but for argument's sake, let's just say there was only one chest of gold. Think about it—not just one gold bar, we are saying a chest full of gold. Now how many of us got a treasure chest of gold at our birth? How many of us got a savings bond at our birth? How many of us got anything at our birth of monetary value? Even if we got one treasure chest of gold at our birth and simply kept it until we were adults, how many of us would consider ourselves to be financially poor at adulthood? What would a treasure chest of gold be worth after thirty years (the age at which Jesus started His ministry)? At this point the argument can, for some, still be made that Jesus was no Bill Gates; however, we should be able to at least not make Him a broke, busted, and disgusted, homeless, barefoot beggar.

Still not able to answer for yourself whether Jesus was financially poor or rich while here on earth? Okay, some of you are probably saying at this point, that it really was not about the money for Jesus and it does not matter whether He was financially rich or not! Correct, you are! Jesus was not concerned about whether He had money or not. Nor should we. Yet, one cannot take away the fact that far too many Christians (and rightly so) still hold to the premise that Christians should be striving to be like Jesus; yet, we cannot reconcile with the Bible what we actually believe about the Bible and Jesus and money. This unfortunately is a topic of much dissension in the body of Christ. Many get very emotionally charged, both ways, when this discussion is raised. That is no reason to run and hide from the discussion. We each must come to own conclusion about Jesus and money.

Why then do we as Christians spend so much time arguing over the fact that Jesus was financially poor? The reason is that this new frontier of practical life teaching, which includes the theology of prosperity, has to spend a lot of time un-teaching and un-doing—erasing, if you will—all the already pre-established status quo, traditionalized theology about Jesus and money that has tainted the minds of Christians. It has led to an abnormal obsession and understanding of what they should know to be the truth about Jesus and money. This pre-established traditional theology has clouded the minds of Christians to the point that they have become victimized by others telling them they are unholy because they have achieved financial success; success that is not celebrated by Jesus because this teaching says that Jesus was financially poor. Pray that the day comes when no discussion centers on Jesus being poor or rich; but until that day comes, we must read the Bible and determine for ourselves whether our Jesus was financially rich or poor while here on earth and not allow others to determine for us who Jesus was as it relates to financial prosperity.

Misconception #2: The Disciples

Who were the disciples? While we know that Jesus had many disciples, it is written that there were twelve very special disciples that lived with Jesus and traveled the country with Jesus for at least three years. Upon closer examination of the disciples, we can begin to see a clearer picture of who Jesus might have been as it relates to His financial abilities. The disciples, contrary to most opinions, were not just everyday average individuals making minimum wage and barely making ends meet. Many times the disciples are depicted as simple fishermen fishing for their daily food. One could easily understand how twelve men who barely had enough to eat, no where permanently to live (no home of their own), and no bright future ahead of them, would gladly follow anyone who promised to take care of them whether the person appeared to have the ability to take care of them or not. In this type of situation, one had little to lose by following anyone wealthy or poor. But how can one begin to fathom how twelve men, highly educated and during quite well financially just give up everything and follow a penniless, homeless, barefoot, beggar of a man called Jesus and actually believe He could take care of all twelve of them when according to some theology He could barely take care of himself?

You have to picture it. Remember, Jesus was fully man, a man like we see everyday. You cannot spiritualize this encounter. Jesus did not make any disciple follow Him; each chose to follow Jesus of their own free will. The disciples were a combination of commercial fishermen, a doctor, and a tax collector. Commercial fishermen own their own boats and have men working for them. These were not individual fishermen with a stick catching enough fish to simply feed their family for the day.

(See Mark 1:14–20.)

The disciple Luke was a physician. While we know that not all doctors are extremely wealthy; most will agree that there are not too many doctors, unless by their own choice, who are struggling to eat, keep a roof over their heads, and pay their bills. Matthew, known as the tax collector, worked for the government—the equivalent of the IRS—collecting taxes from the people. What person in these positions would follow a broke, busted, and barefoot man? Would you? Think about it? If a man that dressed and looked like some of the pictures we have seen of Jesus as broke and barefoot asked you to leave the type of lifestyle of the disciples we just described, would you go? Before you answer that, read Luke 10:2–4 where Jesus tells the disciples they cannot bring anything with them—no money, no traveler's bag, not even an extra pair of shoes. To truly understand this dynamic, bring this up to our generation. You are a doctor living adequately, not even extravagantly, and you are asked this question. You might consider going if you could take your credit cards with you, have access to your own personal bank account, and pack a suitcase of clothes. But, no, Jesus tells you these things cannot go with you. You must leave all. Would you go? Now once again, there are a few of you who are holy enough right now and perhaps are answering, "Sure, I would."

There must be, however, very few of you because the church today is struggling to get individuals to simply give up a few hours each week to come worship and/or volunteer to help do ministry, let alone leave their current jobs and come work for the ministry full-time with no compensation! There are very few individuals today who have a testimony of leaving occupations like this for a ministry. Yes, there are some who work without compensation and volunteer time; however, more often than not, these are individuals who were homemakers, in between jobs, or in low-paying jobs they did not want to work.

Let's paint a different picture. How about if Bill Gates, or Donald Trump, or maybe even Oprah Winfrey call you on the phone, and one of them asked you the same thing? Would you go? For some of us, it would be a no-brainer—we would be on the next plane. Some of us might take a little longer to think about it, and

> **Many Christians believe or have been taught that they are supposed to give everything they receive away in order to be Holy; to keep 'too much' is sinful. How much is too much and who makes that determination?**

some would still say no. But there is a distinct difference here between these two offers. Which offer, or picture of an offer, was painted before the disciples to get twelve men to agree to follow him?

Luke 22:35–36 tells us that Jesus was true to His promise in taking care of the disciples. Jesus is speaking in this passage and it reads, "Then Jesus asked them, 'When I sent you out to preach the Good News and you did not have money, a traveler's bag, or extra clothing, did you lack anything?' 'No,' they replied. 'But now,' he said, 'take your money and a traveler's bag.'" One must ask, where did the money come from and now all the extra clothing requiring a traveler's bag if they started out with nothing and Jesus desired for them to have nothing? Let us also not forget that the disciples said they lacked nothing. How many of us can take care of at least twelve grown men for three years and have them respond that they lacked nothing and have extra now to spare? We must also remember, as articulated earlier, that these twelve were used to living in a decent standard of living. You cannot take care of a person below their certain standard of living and have them respond that they lacked nothing! Is this a broke, busted, and barefoot Jesus who was able to do this?

Please do not trivialize this discussion and go too holy or spiritual and say that Jesus just simply went to the lake and opened a fish's mouth and got money out all the time. Yes, we know and believe that Jesus had a disciple get money on one occasion this way; but wasn't Jesus about showing us that He was just like us and capable of being dependent on the one God for provisions? If every time He needed something, He performed a miracle, He would not be leading by example the life He wanted us to live. Jesus taught about how to live life daily as men on Earth.

We know from Luke 8:3 and many other scriptures that people gave to Jesus and the disciples. That is where the money and other possessions came from. Most do not dispute that fact; but the fact that Jesus may have kept what was given to Him rather than giving it all away is where many will differ in their opinions. Many Christians believe or have been taught that they are supposed to give everything they receive away in order to be Holy; to keep 'too much' is sinful. How much is too much?

We cannot leave our discussion of myths surrounding Jesus and His disciples without talking about Judas. We all know Judas. He is best known for his role in betraying Jesus. But John 12:4–6 tells us that Judas "Was a thief…in charge of the disciples' money, [and] he often stole some for himself." How many of us have a full-time financial advisor or bookkeeper who handles all our money? Why not? For most of us, the answer is because we do not have enough money that would require someone to take care of it. So Judas kept all the money that was used to take care of at least twelve men for three years in a lifestyle that they lacked for nothing (and remember, these were men who were use to eating and sleeping well), and Judas was able to skim off the top, to boot!

Was Jesus financially rich or poor? Not sure, yet? Let us consider Luke 9:10–14. This is the story where Jesus fed the five thousand with five loafs and two fish. But if we take a closer look at verse 13 we can see that prior to Jesus' miracle taking place a discussion on how to feed the crowd took place between Jesus and his disciples. It reads, "But Jesus said, 'You feed them.' Impossible! They protested. We have only five loaves of bread and two fish. Or are you expecting us to go and *buy* enough food for this whole crowd?" (emphasis added.)

Did we just read where a disciple asked Jesus, (and we can assume that it was Judas that asked since he kept all the money) if He wanted them to go and *buy* enough food to feed five thousand hungry people? Do you know how much money it would have taken to feed five thousand people? The text makes clear that this number of five thousand did not include the women and children, just five thousand men. (See verse 14.) I cannot help but raise the question, How many of us can feed five thousand people? Why not? It is important to also point out here that Jesus did not tell them to go look in any fish's mouth for the money to buy the food. The disciple's question is evident enough that the disciples must have had at that point in time enough money to buy food for five thousand people to eat!

Misconception #3: Money Is Evil

We have all heard it. Some of us actually believe it—that money is evil. Many are convinced that the Bible actually says it. First Timothy 6:10 is perhaps one of the most misquoted scriptures. Simply leaving out one word has dramatically changed the meaning of the entire scripture. It reads, "For the love of money is at the root of all kinds of evil. And some people, craving money, have wandered from the faith and pierced themselves with many sorrows." Money, in and of itself, is neither good nor evil. It is what man does, or does not do, with the money that makes it evil. We all know at least one person who is sacrificing his family, his friends, and his life, working himself to death going after financial success. He or she will do anything to get more money. They believe money will address all their problems and make them happy. This is what 1 Timothy is referring to when he speaks of people craving money. At what price are we willing to make such sacrifices—forsaking even Christ and knowing Him better by working all the time and not devoting the time we know we should to study, meditation, and worship?

Last, but certainly not least, we must look at Mark 10:23–25, another oft quoted scripture where Jesus tells the disciples that it is easier for a camel to pass through the eye of a needle than for a rich person to enter the kingdom of heaven. Most people do not realize that the "eye of the needle" is not referring to a sewing needle that we know of today. The eye of a needle in biblical days was a reference to an entrance gate at the wall of a city. The gate, known as the eye of the needle, referred to a smaller gate that required a camel to bend down in order to pass through the opening. This was difficult for a camel to do because of the hump on its back. Therefore, most camels passed through the main gate of a city, which was a larger entrance. Although both were and are difficult to do, the explanation puts the analogy in better perspective of its ability to happen. One can more easily see that a camel can bend down and pass through a smaller gate, than we can ever conceive of a camel actually going through what we now know as the "eye of a needle."

But here in this passage, once again, Jesus is speaking about rich people, a rich man to be exact, who refused to give away his possessions as directed by Jesus. This is the passage that is often used to illustrate the fact that Jesus requires everyone to be poor and give all that they have away in order to go to heaven. However, when reading the Bible, it is important to keep reading an entire chapter or section to understand what is being said. If, therefore, we keep reading this passage, we find these words:

> The disciples were astounded. "Then who in the world can be saved?" they asked.…Jesus replied, "I assure you that everyone who has given up house or brothers or sisters or mother or father or children or property, for my sake and for the Good News, will receive *now* in return a hundred times as many houses, brothers, sisters, mothers, children, and property—along with persecution. *And* in the world to come that person will have eternal life."
> —MARK 10:26, 29–30, EMPHASIS ADDED

Verse 26 must be read again and again, "Then who in the world can be saved?" You must visualize the scenario. Jesus is surrounded by all of His disciples and the rich man talking about material possessions. Jesus tells the rich man to give everything he has away. He, Jesus, then turns to the disciples and tells them how hard it is for rich people to go to heaven; not that rich people cannot go to heaven, but that it is hard for them to get there. The disciples look around at each other and ask, "Who then in the world can be saved?" Did that go over your head? They, the disciples, look around and all they see are rich people, including themselves, which leads them to ask of Jesus, "Well then, who *can* go if rich people can't?"

Jesus responded immediately, making clear it is not about the money but your willingness to give it away when instructed. Jesus clearly says that anyone who gives away anything for His sake or for the Good News will be given back a hundred times that which was given up in this lifetime. Too often we, once again, want to believe all of our rewards are waiting in heaven. It is clear—there is a reward of material possessions if we give up material possessions right now in this lifetime. Jesus is clear as well that we will not just get what we gave up, but one hundred times more than what we gave up. The icing on the cake is that there is still a reward of eternal life after enjoying the benefits of the rewards here in this lifetime.

The focus of all this discussion so far has been to provide a sound, biblical basis for not believing that Jesus was financially poor while here on earth. This discussion is not to prove that He was financially rich either. Rather, this whole dialogue has been to prayerfully open the minds of those who have believed that Jesus was financially poor and therefore have had a warped since of what Christians should be thinking and feeling about money. It will only be at the point that Christians have a healthy understanding of Jesus and His money—or lack thereof, if you still insist on believing that—that we will be able to better see the example Jesus was trying to show us in how to handle financial wealth and prosperity.

Maybe we have believed for so long that Jesus was poor because He did not flaunt the fact that He had wealth. Maybe we believed that Jesus was financially poor because He was always giving to others. But, if He was so poor, where did the possessions come from that He gave? Maybe we believe that He gave away everything He received. That however, would conflict with the role of Judas.

Maybe we believed that Jesus was financially poor because He tells us not to be concerned about gathering material possessions, but instead to focus first on the kingdom of God. (See Matthew 6:31–33.) Why do any of these beliefs have to assume poverty? Can't a person have financial wealth and success, but not flaunt their wealth? Can't they be extremely generous and give away a lot, without being concerned with material possessions?

What do you think?

CHAPTER 2

God's Original Plan for Our Financial Freedom

What was God's original plan for mankind as it relates to financial wealth and freedom? Maybe if we start at the beginning of time and discover what God originally intended for us, we would be better able to understand Christian financial stewardship and prosperity. "In the beginning God created the heavens and the earth." So reads Genesis 1:1. The Book of Genesis tells the creation story that includes the fact that God created everything as He desired the world to be. Chapter 2 of Genesis describes the creation of the Garden of Eden in which God put Adam and Eve to live. The Book of Genesis tells us the Garden of Eden was beautiful and had everything in it that God wanted man and woman to have. The book says there was a large river that flowed through the Garden of Eden. Verses 11 and 12 of chapter 2 of the Book of Genesis also say, "The first branch, called the Pishon, flowed around the entire land of Havilah, where gold is found. The gold of that land is exceptionally pure; aromatic resin and onyx stone are also found there." If God put everything He wanted man to have in the Garden of Eden, why would God put gold—exceptionally pure gold—in the land if He did not want man to have dominion over it? It was only the tree of Good and Evil that was forbidden to Adam and Eve. God did not tell Adam and Eve to leave the gold alone.

> If God put everything He wanted man to have in the Garden of Eden, why would God put gold—exceptionally pure gold—in the garden if He did not want man to have dominion over it?

If the gold was there for Adam and Eve to use, one must ask the question, what happened? Who messed up, that we no longer live with wealth and no lack, as God originally intended? We all know the answer to that—*we messed up!* (See Genesis 3:22–24.)

God then bestowed mercy and grace upon us, and used Abraham to become the father of a great nation who would once again lead his children to the land of no lack. The Book of Genesis chapters 12 and 13 tell the story of the call of Abram. Once again, we hear a lot about Abraham, but we never talk about the fact that Abram was very rich. We hear all that time that God uses the poor, unfortunate people to do His work. In fact, that point is made so much that those with financial wealth or those who have not been homeless, raped, abused, or in some way had a dysfunctional life, believe that God cannot or does not want to use them. Shame on us who preach that gospel—only God can, and does, use anyone He chooses, regardless of whether they are wealthy or poor.

We rarely hear that God also uses those of substantial wealth. Why is that? If the truth would be told, it would probably be because there are more broke folks who can identify with the first type of teaching and preaching than there are financially stable folks. Or maybe it is because the same emotional reaction cannot be had from a crowd when talking about using those of substantial wealth. There are so few of them. No one shouts, dances, or gets more emotional than when a preacher talks about God using the less-than for His work. It becomes like a badge of honor to have been broke, busted, and disgusted at some point in your life. It seems as if it is ungodly to have been born into a loving family, with godly morals and values, not on the brink of poverty, and loves the Lord. Yet, there are many, many examples of those of substantial wealth whom God used in the Bible. Genesis 12:5 says that when Abram left, "He took his wife, Sarai, his nephew Lot, and all his *wealth*" (emphasis added.) Genesis 13:1–2 says, "So Abram left Egypt and traveled north into the Negev, along with his wife and Lot and all that they owned. (Abram was *very rich in livestock, silver, and gold.),*" (emphasis added.) It is clear that Abram was not only spiritually rich, but financially rich. If you continue to read the story of Abram, you will find that God blessed him to become even richer. In Genesis 15:13–14, God repeats the promise He made to Abram with these words, "Then the LORD said to Abram, 'You can be sure that your descendants will be strangers in a foreign land, where they will be oppressed as slaves for 400 years. But I will punish the nation that enslaves them, and in the end they will come away with *great wealth*,'" (emphasis added.)

We all know how the story goes—the children of Abraham (through Isaac and Jacob) go into bondage in the land of Egypt and God sends Moses to deliver them from the wrath of Pharaoh. Pharaoh is stubborn, however, and it is not until the firstborn of both animal and man dies that Pharaoh lets the children of Israel go. Once again, everything about this story is preached and taught, especially during the Easter or Resurrection season of early Spring. The one thing that is most often left out of the story is that the children of Israel did not leave as poor, destitute slaves. In Exodus 12:35–36 we read:

> And the people of Israel did as Moses had instructed; they asked the Egyptians for clothing and articles of silver and gold. The LORD caused the Egyptians to look favorably on the Israelites, and they gave the Israelites whatever they asked for. So they stripped the Egyptians of their wealth!

If God did not desire for us to have gold and silver and financial wealth, why did He instruct the Israelites to make sure they had plenty of it before they left Egypt? Why did God soften the hearts of the Egyptians to ensure that they gave the Israelites all that they asked for? God could have simply told them to get food and water. In fact, God could have told them to take nothing with them for He would provide! Just like the Garden of Eden, it was God's original plan that man would have financial freedom—gold and silver, livestock, and plenty of clothing.

But once again, *who messed up?* If you do not know that answer, then continue reading the story of the children of Israel and their trials through the wilderness. God told Moses to join Him on Mount Sinai where He could give Moses additional instructions about how the people are to live and worship Him. But Moses took too long for the people of Israel. They went to Aaron and got him to build them a calf made of the gold that they had just gotten from the Egyptians because of God's divine grace to bestow such wealth upon them upon leaving bondage. This infuriated God and Moses, for God did not give them the gold to build an idol. Genesis 32:26 tells us that God instructed Moses to stand at the entrance of the camp and instructed everyone who was on the Lord's side to join him. The scripture says, "And all the Levites came." This is an important point that will be discussed in greater detail in a later chapter. The Levites were then instructed to strap on their swords and kill everyone who was not on their side. The Levites had to kill their own mothers, fathers, brothers, and sisters. More than three thousand people were killed that day. Moses then told all the Levites, in Exodus 32:29, "Today you have been ordained for the service of the Lord, for you obeyed him even though it meant killing your own sons and brothers. Because of this, he will now give you a great blessing."

So who messed up? Once again, we messed up! God did not tell the children of Israel to get the gold to be misused as it was. God gave us a plan for how

He wanted the money and possessions He provided to us to be used. Yet, over and over again, we decide that *we want* to use it how we want to use it and not how God had intended!

When will we learn the lesson that the money and possessions are not the problem or issue? What we do with the money and possessions outside of God's will is the problem. If we do not do with it what He intended, or if we mess up, we will be punished. We will not have peace of mind, we will not have peace in our homes, and our money will disappear as if we have holes in our pockets.

The children of Israel wandered through the wilderness for forty years because of their disobedience. They were on their way to the land of Canaan where nothing was lacking. Yet their disobedience caused many of them to never see the Promised Land.

What was God's original plan? The Garden of Eden, and then the land of Canaan. Deuteronomy 8 best describes the land of Canaan and what God expects from us in return for receiving the blessing of a land of Canaan. Verses 1 through 5 of chapter 8 of the Book of Deuteronomy have Moses reminding the children of Israel of all that God has done for them the last forty years while they had been wandering through the wilderness. Moses is reminding them to obey God and all of His commands if they want to stay and enjoy the land of Canaan. He is reminding them of their past and not to repeat the sins of the past, for they know those sins will cause them to mess up. Deuteronomy 8:6 clearly spells out like no other scriptures what God's plan was for our lives—our financial lives, our lifestyle, and our possessions. It reads:

> So obey the commands of the Lord your God by walking in his ways and *fearing* him. For the Lord your God is bringing you into a good land of flowing streams and pools of water, with springs that gush forth in the valleys and hills. It is a land of wheat and barley, of grapevines, fig trees, pomegranates, olives, and honey. It is a land where food is plentiful and nothing is lacking. It is a land where iron is as common as stone, and copper is abundant in the hills. When you have eaten your fill, praise the Lord your God for the good land he has given you. But that is the time to be careful! Beware that in your plenty you do not forget the Lord your God and disobey his commands, regulations, and laws. For when you have become full and prosperous and have built fine homes to live in, and when your flocks and herds have become very large and your silver and gold have multiplied along with everything else, that is the time to be careful. Do not become proud at that time and forget the Lord your God, who rescued

you from slavery in the land of Egypt....He
did it so you would never think that it was
your own strength and energy that made you
wealthy. Always remember that it is the Lord
your God who gives you power to become
rich, and he does it to fulfill the covenant he
made with your ancestors with an oath.

—DEUTERONOMY 8:6–14, 17–18,
EMPHASIS ADDED

What was God's original plan—the second
time—after *we messed* up the Garden of Eden? God
tried one more time to put us in another Garden of
Eden, the land of Canaan, where according to Deuteronomy 8 nothing was lacking. All the good food
we could imagine was there, and in plenty. God tells
the people to eat until they are full—there is nothing wrong with that. God tells the people to build
their fine homes to live in—there is nothing wrong
with that. God tells the people that their flocks and
herds will multiply and become very large—there
is nothing wrong with that. God tells the people
that their gold and silver will multiply along with
everything else—there is nothing wrong with that.
God tells the people that they will become wealthy
and rich—there is nothing wrong with that! If
God does not have a problem with us having these
things—in fact, He makes it clear that He is giving
these things to us—then why does man have such a

problem with it when someone possesses it?

This was God's original plan! Deuteronomy 8 tells me that it is okay to live in a big, fancy, house. It tells me it is okay to have more than one car, and a nice, expensive car, too (as in, flocks and herds). It tells me it is okay to have a lot of money in the bank (gold and silver). So what is the problem? Maybe it is because:

> We do not understand the Bible.

> We do not read the Bible.

> We believe what others say negatively about the Bible and wealth.

> We are jealous and envious of what others have.

> We do not believe the Bible.

> We do not understand why we do not have the wealth personally, and yet we go to church everyday and say that we are saved.

> Or, for too long we have been mis-educated about money and the Bible.

God makes it clear that we must obey Him and His commands in order to enjoy the land of Canaan in our lives. He makes it clear that He has no problem with our having financial success in our lives; just do what He tells you to do. Are you doing what He tells you to do—*or are you messing up?*

We know how the story ends for those in the land of Canaan. They messed up! God had to send another nation in to conquer them, because they refused to obey Him. God has tried twice to put us in a land where nothing is lacking—and each time who messed up? We messed up! God is here now for the third time through His Son, Jesus. Jesus said He came so that we might have life and have it more abundantly. We must learn what God/Jesus expects of us if we are not to mess up. How does God want us to live with the finances He provides for us?

Last, and certainly not least, to understand God's original plan for our financial freedom, we need only look to the description of heaven. Revelation 21:18–21 says:

> The wall was made of jasper, and the city was pure gold, as clear as glass. The wall of the city was built on foundation stones inlaid with twelve precious stones: the first was jasper, the second sapphire, the third agate, the fourth emerald, the fifth onyx, the sixth carnelian, the seventh chrysolite, the eighth beryl, the ninth topaz, the tenth chrysoprase, the eleventh jacinth, the twelfth amethyst. The twelve gates

> were made of pearls—each gate from a single
> pearl! And the main street was pure gold, as
> clear as glass.

How can a God who is so opposed to wealth, opulence, and gold (if that is what you *still* believe) have His home made that way? This is the home that Jesus said He left us here on Earth to go back to and to prepare a place for us. In fact, Jesus' very words were "in my Father's house are many mansions" (John 14:2, KJV). *Webster's Dictionary* defines a mansion as a "large imposing residence."[1] Why has Jesus gone to prepare a mansion for us if He is opposed to such styles of living? Most of us are afraid to leave anyone alone in our own homes of wealth with someone who has never experienced or understood wealth for fear of them stealing something. God might need to keep guards watching some of us who make it to heaven because we might be trying to dig out a pearl from the gate or cut a bar of gold from the streets. Why would God want us to live in lack here on Earth never experiencing such a lifestyle, only to take us to such a lifestyle after death? It simply does not add up. God is not hypocritical. God would not say one thing, and then do another thing. What does add up and does not conflict with the Bible is:

God is the Creator of wealth and decides to whom He will bless with the ability to have wealth.

God's original plan and His current plan is for His children to inherit the blessing of living in the Garden of Eden, the land of Canaan, and the land of no lack right here on Earth.

God simply asks that His children not get the big head, to begin to think that they achieved on their own.

God simply asks that His children obey all His commands and worship Him.

Jesus instructs us not to be overly concerned with securing wealth or material possessions, but to first seek God, learn all about Him, love Him, obey His commands, and then God will give us everything else we need or desire. (See Matthew 6:33.) If God's original plan was that we would have and possess wealth, there must have been a purpose in His plan for our use of this wealth. Why would God need the children of Israel to take gold with them when they left Egypt? Why would God bless Christians to become wealthy as articulated in Deuteronomy 8? The following purposes can be supported biblically and should be studied and adopted as principles by which a Christian ought to live with God-given wealth. In order of importance, they are:

To build the Temple of God (churches, synagogues)

We have previously discussed the Exodus of the children of Israel where God commanded the Israelites to ask the Egyptians to give to them all the gold, silver, and clothing that they could take with them. God had softened the hearts of the Egyptians and the Israelites left with great wealth. The entire chapter of Exodus 35 tells the commands from God to Moses about constructing the temple of God; a house of worship. In verse 4 of that chapter we find that Moses told the people to bring their offerings of "gold, silver, bronze, blue, purple, and scarlet yarn; fine linen; goat hair for cloth; tanned ram skins and fine goatskin leather; acacia wood; olive oil for lamps; spices for the anointing oil and the fragrant incense; onyx stones, and other stones to be set in the ephod and the chest piece." It is quite obvious from this passage that God *gave* the Israelites these possessions to *give back* a portion for the construction of the temple. How else would God have commanded the Israelites to give something that conceivably they did not have nor possess as slaves; nor any way of getting them? Only God could have the foresight to have known that He wanted the Israelites to be able to build a Temple of His desire that required gold, silver, and other fine and precious stones and cloths.

Two important points can be made here. One point is that God *gives* to us so that we have it when He needs us to do with it what He desires. The second point helps to further our understanding of the Bible and money or wealth. How can a God who is so opposed to opulence demand that the Temple be built with such opulence? Why is there so much said today about how much is spent by churches building God's house? Why wouldn't a ministry want to build the best for God that they can afford? Chapter 36 of the Book of Exodus describes in very specific details the beauty of the Temple with posts that are overlaid in gold, utensils made of gold, and fine linen for table coverings.

For Christians today, it is still God's desire that we bring our gifts to the Temple so that it can be constructed and maintained with the same opulence as described here. It is a sad commentary to see the state of condition of many of the churches around America and the world. Who would want to join a run-down, doors-hanging-off-the-hinges, paint-chipping, walkway-cracked, carpet-dirty-and-torn, pews-worn-out church? Is this the example any Christian wants to show of a God we profess to provide all our needs? It is no wonder the world does not want to become a Christian. They look and say that they can take better care of themselves than this God we are exemplifying!

Jesus, as one of His last commands, instructed us to go out into all the world making disciples. Unfortunately, it takes money, and a lot of it, to spread the Gospel throughout the world today. Missionaries have to have plane tickets to travel and per diems from which to live. Radio and television broadcast time can cost ministries millions of dollars. Although volunteers help tremendously in administering many programs, it still takes money to purchase or lease the buildings that house programs such as food banks, clothing stores, shelters for abused women and children, and homeless families. These facilities also have utility bills to pay and, in many cases, must employ at least one or two full-time individuals. Effective ministries simply are not cheap. Today many Christians need counseling to deal with issues of abuse as a child, neglect, family dysfunctions, pain of divorce, and many of the once hidden problems that are now in the forefront of America. It takes money to support these much needed ministries. It is no longer acceptable for an untrained, but loving church mom to counsel church members. It requires trained, degreed individuals, in most cases, that are not volunteers but paid staff. Our society, unfortunately, is a lawsuit happy society. The church must protect itself and provide competent staff and sufficient insurance coverage (which takes money) to provide for ministry needs.

To give Christians a voice and authority

Ecclesiastes 9:13–16 reads, "Here is another bit of wisdom that has impressed me as I have watched the way our world works. There was a small town with only a few people, and a great king came with his army and besieged it. A poor, wise man knew how to save the town, and so it was rescued. But afterward no one thought to thank him. So even though wisdom is better than strength, those who are wise will be despised if they are poor. What they say will not be appreciated for long."

No passage of scripture more clearly articulates the way the world works. No one listens to the poor person! They can be the wisest person in the world with all the right answers but no one will follow them! How many of you will take the financial advice of a homeless person about how to invest your money? Why not? How many of you on the other hand, will readily take advice from Donald Trump? What preacher did President Bill Clinton call upon when he got into spiritual trouble? What preacher does any president call upon when they need spiritual advice? Who ministers to Oprah? Who ministers to Bill Gates? Who ministers to the Kennedys? Do you get the picture? Someone, some preacher, has to minister to them. Do you think any of them call upon the broke and busted preacher? No, for a number of reasons! One reason is because they simply do not know the broke preachers! These broke preachers do not travel in their circles! It does not make the broke preacher any less qualified to minister to them; but the reality is, they simply do not have a voice of authority—they are not known!

Many of these wealthy individuals would be scared to death that these broke preachers would simply be trying to get them to give some money to their cause. These broke preachers cannot call up any of these influential individuals and get an appointment as easily as a well-known affluent preacher can. The reality exists that these wealthy individuals also need someone who can minister to them. Just like most people would not take the financial advice from a homeless individual, most wealthy people will not even sit at the table of a broke preacher to entertain a conversation about anything of value to the kingdom of God. Therefore God had to make wealthy preachers. We all can name many wealthy and influential preachers who are in a position to minister to unsaved politicians, celebrities, and other wealthy people. Christians have to be at the table in order to influence the world. Unfortunately, in our society that sometimes requires wealth and influence. It is no wonder that rap stars have the ear of young teens. Rap stars have the wealth to control what is shown on television, what is sold in stores, what is heard on the radio.

When will Christians start controlling anything? When will we stop fighting each other and start fighting the real enemy? We are killing our witness with our infighting! When will we begin to believe the Bible when it clearly says in Genesis and throughout the Bible that it was God's original plan that Christians controlled the world.

Instead, we are infighting about the wealth of each other! How sad. No one sees Oprah complaining about how much money Katie Couric makes. No one sees programs complaining about how the world lives in such opulence. In fact, there are several shows that proudly give tours into the homes of the rich and famous. Many people watch and admire these individuals for what they have achieved. Yet if the home of a prosperous preacher was included in such a show, the rest of the talk shows across the world would talk about their "disgust" of the display and disgrace of such living. I just do not understand it! It cannot be about the work ethic. Most preachers work long hours, seven days a week. They, like most doctors, are always on call. It is one of the most demanding professions!

To personally enjoy

Although the Bible is clear that we are to enjoy the fruits of our labor as it is a gift from God (See Ecclesiastes 3:13), this purpose is taken out of order of priority and is perhaps what has caused many in the Christian faith to stumble. The question of how much we are to keep and enjoy for ourselves is at the root of much Christian debates. How much is too much to keep? How much should a Christian give away? Paul in 2 Corinthians 8:12–13 says, "Whatever you give is acceptable if you give it eagerly. And give according to what you have, not what you don't have. Of course, I don't mean your giving should make life easy for others and hard for yourselves. I only mean that there should be some equality."

Paul is speaking clearly that God really does not care about the money. God is focused on your heart and your willing desire to give. God does not require, contrary to popular opinion, that an individual give away all that he has or to suffer lack. Even when Jesus in Luke 18:18–29, the parable of the rich man, tells the man to sell all his goods and follow him, Jesus was not making a statement to infer that everyone must do that in order to go to heaven. Jesus was clearly making a point that an individual cannot love his money more than he loves obeying the commands of Him (Jesus). Once again, 1 Timothy 6:10 reminds us that it is the love of money that is at the root of God's disappointment in us; not us having the money.

This point is further illustrated in Luke 19:1–10. This is the passage about Jesus and Zacchaeus. Zacchaeus was an influential and wealthy tax collector who climbed a tree to see Jesus because of the crowds and the fact that he was too short to see over the crowds. When Jesus saw how hard Zacchaeus had tried just to see Him, Jesus spoke to Zacchaeus and told Him that he would go home with him for dinner. It was after this that Zacchaeus told Jesus he would give away half of his wealth to the poor and repay anyone four times what he owed them if he overcharged them. "Jesus responded, 'Salvation has come to this home today, for this man has shown himself to be a true son of Abraham. For the Son of Man came to seek and save those who are lost'" (Luke 19:9–10). If poverty and the giving away of all that one has is what Jesus desires, how is it that He is proud of Zacchaeus when all he gave away was half of his money? Would Jesus not have told him, "I'm sorry, Zacchaeus, but you must give away all, not just half." The Bible does not say how wealthy Zacchaeus was, but what if by our standards, Zacchaeus was a billionaire. Even if he gave away half of his money, his lifestyle would still be that of the rich and famous; a very opulent lifestyle. If Zacchaeus then became a Christian and, heaven forbid, a preacher, society would talk negatively about his lifestyle!

The parable of the talents (Matt. 25:14–30) and the parable of the ten servants (Luke 19:11–26) tell the story of God's disappointment in people who are given money and they are not good stewards of the money. Being a good steward over the money in each of these parables, were described as taking the money and investing it to make more money. In Luke 19:22, the steward is scolded for not at least putting the money in the bank and letting it earn interest. In neither of these parables, does the Owner (God) tell the servants to simply give all the money away! Proverbs 27:18 says, "As workers who tend a fig tree are allowed to eat the fruit, so workers who protect their employer's interests will be rewarded." God is our Employer as we are His workers in the vineyard. Therefore, it would seem reasonable according to this passage from Proverbs that God would reward those of us who are good workers. Are we required to hide what God has given to us as our reward for fear of what others will say or think?

So, how much is too much to keep? Using these three purposes for our finances discussed above, we can begin to bring together a plan or spending budget to govern how we manage what God has given us.

CHAPTER 3

Managing Our Money God's Way

To understand how to manage our money God's way, we must understand the differences between our needs, wants, and desires. In addition, we must understand the biblical teachings on tithes, paying ourselves, paying our obligations, and giving to others.

Here is how one should strive to live on their money:

10 percent	Tithes
10 percent	Pay yourself (save)
70 percent	Pay obligations (to enjoy)
10 percent	Give to others (offerings)
100 percent	Total income

Everyone should strive to live on 70 percent of the money they earn. If everyone lived on 70 percent of their money, there would never be a financial crisis in the world. If everyone paid their tithes, the Gospel of Jesus Christ would be able to be taught throughout the world. If everyone paid their tithes, the church could become the voice of the world; the authority that God had originally planned for it to be to influence society. If everyone gave away another 10 percent of their income; there would be no world hunger; no homelessness; no lack of resources needed to address many of the ills of our society.

It is not impossible to do. Unfortunately, many are not taught these principles of financial living until well after they are already way over their heads in debt and trying to make ends meet. Many are never taught the difference between our needs, wants, and desires. For those few who will admit they knew the difference, some will have to admit that they were taught to get what you want, not what you need. So when the first job came along, you got what you wanted—not the starter car, but the luxury SUV—after all, you deserved it! With the new job came a credit card in the mail! You never even had to apply, you were pre-approved! The credit card allowed you the freedom to buy items you wanted—but not necessarily needed—immediately. You did not have to wait until payday. Of course, you also had to have the cell phone. And not just any cell phone, you had to have the latest camera phone with text messaging and internet access.

Now, all of a sudden, you are grown up and you want your own space—your own apartment. Never once did you stop to think about the fact that while you were buying all this stuff, mom and dad were paying the rent or mortgage. But you were an adult, so you left and got your own place. Then all the bills came due at the same time, and that paycheck that you thought would pay the bills suddenly was not enough. You forgot about all the charges you had made on your credit card—all the clothes and the restaurant bills. You pay the minimum due on the credit card now because you cannot afford to pay off the entire balance. Then the car needs an oil change and new tires. Taxes are due, your insurance went up—suddenly, all the unexpected bills start to show up. On top of all of that you get sick, and because you are new on your job you do not have sick leave, so your paycheck is reduced as a result of absences.

Before you know it, stacked on the kitchen cabinet or stuffed in some drawer, are all the utility bills, cell phone bills, and past due notices that are now overwhelming! You cannot pay them because you never saved a dime! You never thought that you would get sick, that the car would eventually need new tires, or that you would get laid off from your job! You took care of your wants and desires before you took care of your needs.

Needs, Wants, and Desires

Many failed to learn the difference between *needs*, *wants*, and *desires* in life. The sooner this lesson is learned; the sooner individuals will be able to truly understand God's plan for their finances and enjoy the fruits of their labor.

Few will disagree that there is a difference between needs, wants, and desires in life. However, most will argue with the order of priority in obtaining your needs, wants, and desires in life. For purposes of this discussion, the following definitions will be used:

> *Needs*: basic necessities to sustain life, including food, clothing, shelter, and transportation
>
> *Wants*: necessities for a comfortable lifestyle
>
> *Desires*: luxuries in life

A cursory review of the definitions appears to indicate that all three terms mean the same thing—items needed to survive. However, upon closer examination, one can see that each term has a distinctly different definition. Your needs are the bare minimum you must have in order to live. Everyone must eat something, have some type of clothing to protect us from the weather, somewhere to live to also protect us from the weather, and some sort of transportation to get back and forth to work if we are not blessed to be able to walk to work or catch public transportation. In your needs stage, eating can be as simple and inexpensive as peanut butter and jelly sandwiches, canned soup, hamburger helper, and oatmeal. Clothing can be as simple and inexpensive as two pair of shoes: one to wear to church, work, or other formal events, and one pair to play in or put on when not going to the formal events; two pair of pants, two shirts, one pair of jeans, one pair of sneakers, one dress, maybe two, and for men, one nice suit with two different shirts and ties to mix and match with the suit.

Remember those days? There were no long decisions in the morning about what to wear. You did not have to get up an hour early to get ready. You could sleep up to thirty minutes before it was time to leave and be out of the house. Then when you left the house you either walked to the bus stop to catch the bus to work, to the subway to catch the train, or wait for the neighbor who was the carpool driver for the week. Transportation was, if you were fortunate enough, one car for a family. The car was not the latest model car nor the largest or most expensive, but it was a reliable car that was economical on gas and would not break down.

Shelter from the weather, or what you would call home might have been living with the parents until you could afford a place of your own, or living in a studio apartment, a one-bedroom apartment, or a simple modest home where siblings shared bedrooms and one bathroom was shared by all who lived in the home.

These represent our basic needs in order to live a productive life in society. It does not take a lot of money to simply live. Many families have lived on one paycheck and have never lacked a roof over their heads nor food on the table. Many of these same families were able to send their children to college without the assistance of financial aid or student loans. Many of these families had outstanding credit scores, always paid their bills on time, never filed for bankruptcy, and had money in the bank for emergencies. How were they able to do it? They learned the secret early to enjoying a life free from unnecessary financial stress.

What is the secret? The secret is simple. Take care of your basic needs before you move to your wants in life, and before you move to your desires in life. Basic needs include having a savings account to take care of unexpected financial situations or future goals such as retirement or college for your children.

The next step after understanding the difference between your needs, wants, and desires is to be honest with yourself. Too many people say one thing and then do another. What you say is important to you must line up with your actions. If you say you love Jesus, then your actions should show that you love Jesus. What does that have to do with finances?

> **God's first priority for your money is to pay your tithes—to build the Temple of God.**

If you say your goal is to reduce your debt so that you can afford to tithe, then is having a cell phone or cable service really a need? Or is it a desire? Do you have to drive the SUV, or will a smaller, economical car do just as well? Why are you driving the luxury SUV? Because you can easily afford the payments? Or are you trying to impress and keep up with the Jones? Do you really need the five-bedroom house or will a three-bedroom serve you just as well? Is your closet so packed with clothes that you need to move to a larger house with a larger closet so you can buy more clothes?

Anyone who lives in America knows the American dream is to have the opportunity to prosper on their own terms and do whatever their heart desires, which may also include having a life filled with luxury items. Is anything wrong with owning any of these things? Your answer will depend on your interpretation of money and the Bible. By now, you should know that there is nothing wrong in and of itself with having these things. What is wrong is not being able to honor your word and pay your obligations! What is wrong is not saving some money for emergencies, but instead relying on others to bail you out financially because you have overextended your finances! We are not talking about extenuating circumstances such as prolonged illnesses, or fixed income senior citizens, or even the truly poor who are not able to work. What is wrong is not taking care of your basic needs before buying your wants and desires (God's way).

Pay Your Tithes

If we pay our tithes first, then the scripture tells us that we will have the beginning of knowledge, wisdom, and discipline to make good decisions about how to spend the rest of our money. This is where the majority of people fail in their stewardship. They have failed to seek God and gain the discipline and wisdom to know how to spend the rest of their money.

As discussed earlier, God's first and highest priority for blessing Christians with finances is to finance

His church and to spread the gospel throughout the world. The biblical basis for supporting the church is through tithes and offerings. All Christians who desire to live the principles of managing money God's way must first pay their tithes and offerings. Deuteronomy 14:22–23 says (emphasis added):

> You must set aside a tithe of your crops—one-tenth of all the crops you harvest each year. Bring this tithe to the place the Lord your God chooses for his name to be honored, and eat it there in his presence. This applies to your tithes of grain, new wine, olive oil, and the firstborn males of your flocks and herds. The purpose of tithing is to teach you always to *fear* the Lord your God.

From this Old Testament scripture, we find that:

> 1. A tithe is one-tenth of your crops, or that which you harvest. In modern terms, it represents your earnings, wages, investments, and other income. Therefore, we should be giving 10 percent of our income each year.
>
> 2. Bring your tithes to the place God chooses for His name to be honored—

church and worship services. The question is also often asked whether or not giving to other charitable organizations such as the United Way or Goodwill counts toward the tithe. This passage says that the tithe should be brought to the place where the Lord chose for His name to be honored. We know that the place the Lord chose for His name to be honored was the temple or modern day church. We find this supported by 2 Samuel 7:13 where it reads, "He is the one who will build a house—a temple—for my name." This is the passage where King David wanted to build the Temple for God's name to be honored. However, God instructed King David that he would not be allowed to build the temple but that his son, Solomon, would be allowed to build the temple of God.

3. The purpose of tithing is to teach you to fear the Lord. So often we are taught the only reason we tithe is to receive blessings. Yet, this passage says that God will know if we fear Him by whether we tithe or not. Reading this scripture makes us think about personal creditors.

Why do you pay them each month? The answer is simple. You pay them because you fear what they can do to you if you do not pay them. There is a direct correlation between not paying the electric bill and the ability to have lights when you enter your home. You know for a fact the end result of not paying a creditor. The same applies to whether you pay your mortgage, or your car note. If you want a home that has not been padlocked, or a car that has not been repossessed, you will pay the bill. But what about God's bill (tithe)? Can we make a direct correlation between not paying our tithes and something that happens in our lives? If we have a flat tire, do we ever say, "Man, if I had paid my tithes, I would not have a flat tire." Do we ever blame our lack of tithing on anything that happens in our life? That is the problem—we really do not believe things happening in our lives are directly related to our not tithing. That is primarily because the result of not tithing is different for each of us. That makes it difficult for us to know for sure that "things happened" because of not tithing. If the Bible said that if we did

not tithe we would never have children,
or never have a happy marriage, or never
have a good job, we would tithe in a
heartbeat.

We have heard preachers use the saying, "Pay me
now or pay me later," as it relates to non-tithing. How
often do we attribute unexpected outflows of money to
our not tithing? Is it really God getting His tithe that
way, trying to teach us a lesson? Would our God really
do that? Malachi 3:8–10 says that God really would
do that. It reads:

> Should people cheat God? Yet you have
> cheated me! But you ask, "What do you
> mean? When did we ever cheat you?" You
> have cheated me of the tithes and offerings
> due to me. You are under a curse, for your
> whole nation has been cheating me. Bring
> all the tithes into the storehouse so there
> will be enough food in my Temple.

Look at everything these scriptures teach on
tithes and offerings:

We should be bringing our tithes and offerings to the "storehouse."

What is the "storehouse?" A storehouse is a place
where one stores food so that they can retrieve the
food when needed at a later time. Where are you

as a Christian fed and what do you eat? Our food should be the Word of God, for we know that Jesus said to Satan, "People need more than bread for their life; they must feed on every word of God" (Matt. 4:4, author's paraphrase). Where do you as a Christian receive the Word of God, or your food? Most Christians receive the majority of their meals from a local church. Therefore, your tithes should be taken to your local church. This does not negate the fact that we all eat out sometimes. Giving to other churches or ministries, whether local, national, or international, is not wrong. In fact, it is encouraged. However, you should not be giving these ministries your tithes. They should receive your offerings.

Tithes and offerings are a command from God.

The passage says that your tithes are "due" to God. It is not negotiable. Very few Christians will argue the fact that we all should still be obeying the Ten Commandments, if not everything that is written in the Old Testament. Which commandment deals with tithing? "Thou shalt not steal," is the commandment that directly ties back into Malachi 3:10, and therefore should be obeyed by all who are Christians.

If you follow the commands, you will be blessed.

We need only to continue reading Malachi 3:10–11 where God says, "If you do [bring your tithes]…I will open the windows of heaven for you. I will pour out a blessing so great you won't have enough room to take it in! Try it! Put Me to the test! Your crops will be abundant, for I will guard them from insects and disease."

Most Christians are taught that they tithe to get a blessing. That is why you have so many disappointed Christians who misunderstand the concept of tithing. You tithe to show God that you fear Him! However, the result of tithing is that you will be blessed. Here's an analogy. The Bible is clear that God is our Father and we are His children. Most children have household chores and responsibilities that they have to do. It is a command from their parents.

Suppose you have a child who comes to you and asks you for an extra ten dollars to go to the movies with some friends. You, as the parent, have several responses you could give your child. If your child has been obedient and done all that you have asked (chores and responsibilities) and if you have the money you will probably give it to the child, simply because they are good and obedient children. But if your child has not done what they were supposed to do (tithes), you might,

> **You do not tithe to get a blessing! Blessings are the result of tithing!**

54

as a parent, say no because they have been disobedient. Few would argue with that parenting guideline. Why would you think, God, our Father, is any different when He decides whether to give us something we ask for or not? What if on the other hand, your child had been obedient and done all they were suppose to do, but you still said no to their request and their response back to you was, "That's not fair; I did everything I was suppose to do (tithes)! I cleaned my room, I make good grades in school." What is the response of most parents? Perhaps something like, "What do you mean, not fair? I do not owe you anything extra. You are supposed to clean your room, make good grades, and do what I ask of you as your parent!"

That is exactly the way God may feel, when Christians go to the altars on Sunday and weep and cry to God about things they want and end their prayer with, "I paid my tithes so I am expecting a blessing!" God is probably sitting in heaven saying, *What do you mean I am obligated because you paid your tithes? You are supposed to pay your tithes. I do not have to do anything, and if you are paying your tithes simply to get something, then you are doing it for the wrong reasons and nothing is coming!*

We must remember, God knows our pure intent for He can see our hearts. Tithing is a matter of the heart and we do it because we love God and want to be obedient children.

If you do not follow the commands, you will be cursed.

There is one final point on the purpose of *fear* and its connection to God. Proverbs 1:7 says the, "*fear* of the LORD is the foundation of true knowledge, but fools despise wisdom and discipline" (emphasis added). It takes discipline to tithe. According to *Webster's Dictionary*, discipline is "a training that corrects, molds, or perfects the mental faculties or moral character of an individual by enforcing obedience."[1] Therefore, without discipline, you cannot tithe.

It is no wonder that so many Christians are one paycheck away from financial disaster. They are not disciplined in their life. They have not learned to be disciplined in their spending. They have no wisdom when it comes to making good decisions about what to buy and what not to buy. They cannot discipline themselves to keep from making impulsive buying decisions.

> **Grace and the New Testament is not an excuse to do what we want to do, but to do what is pleasing to God.**

If you do not tithe, according to the scripture, you do not fear the Lord. If you do not fear the Lord, you cannot gain the knowledge God so desperately wants us to achieve. Without the knowledge of God, we cannot have the "keys of the Kingdom" (Matt. 16:19) here on earth, for, "My people are destroyed for lack of knowledge" says the Lord (Hosea 4:6, KJV).

Remember, blessings from God come in all forms, shapes, and sizes. Blessings will not necessarily be monetary. Blessings can be a great marriage, great health, loving families, children, great jobs, homes, peace of mind, and contentment. Increase your prayer life and ask God to show you where you may be disobedient to His desire with regard to your giving.

Here is where some Christians raise the question as to whether we have to tithe, since tithing has been previously taught as only under the Law of Moses (Old Testament) from which the New Testament (grace) frees us. There are several places in the Bible in both the Old and New Testaments that support tithing. Tithing is not limited to the Laws of Moses. The Law of Moses was given as written in the Book of Exodus beginning around chapter 20. However, tithing is mentioned even before the Law of Moses was given by God. In Genesis 14:20, we find that tithes were first mentioned when Abram, "gave Melchizedek a tenth [a tithe] of all the goods he had recovered." Abram gave these tithes to Melchizedek, who was King of Salem and a priest of God Most

High, when Melchizedek brought Abram bread and wine and pronounced a blessing on Abram's life. The tithes Abram gave to Melchizedek represented 10 percent of all the spoils of war he had just received. This happened clearly before the Laws of Moses were revealed by God.

We can also refer to Genesis 28:22 where Jacob declared, "I will present to God a tenth of everything he gives me." Jacob made this declaration because he had just had a revelation from God about the blessings God was about to place upon his life. This was also before the Law of Moses as recorded in Exodus. Grace is not an excuse to do what we want to do, but to do what is pleasing to God. In Hebrews 8:10 we find God speaking these words:

> But this is the new covenant I will make with the people of Israel on that day, says the LORD: I will put my laws in their minds, and I will write them on their hearts.

So how can these two individuals, Jacob and Abram, who were alive before the Law of Moses, know about giving one-tenth of what they have to God or His representative? The same way Christians freed from the Laws of Moses, and living under grace, know about giving one-tenth of what they have to God or His representative. The Spirit of God revealed to them the giving of tithes through their hearts. But for those Christians who must still see tithing in the New Testament, there are scriptures such as Matthew 23:23 that also support tithing:

> What sorrow awaits you teachers of religious law and you Pharisees. Hypocrites! For you are careful to tithe even the tiniest income from your herb gardens, but you ignore the more important aspects of the law—justice, mercy, and faith. You should tithe, yes, but do not neglect the more important things.

Here Jesus is speaking to the Pharisees and clearly He says that you *should* tithe. It is repeated again in Luke 11:42. We also find in Matthew 5:17–20 (emphasis added) Jesus saying:

> Don't misunderstand why I have come. I did not come to abolish the law of Moses or the writings of the prophets. No, I came to accomplish their purpose. I tell you the truth, until heaven and earth disappear, not *even the smallest detail of God's law will disappear until its purpose is achieved.* So if you ignore the least commandment and teach others to do the same, you will be called the least in the Kingdom of Heaven. But anyone who obeys God's laws and teaches them will be called great in the Kingdom of Heaven. But I warn you—unless your righteousness is better than

the righteousness of the teachers of religious law and the Pharisees, you will never enter the Kingdom of Heaven!

Since God's law will remain until its purpose is achieved, we must once again go back to the purpose of tithing. The purpose of tithing is to teach us to *fear* God and to provide for the storehouse—the church. Have these purposes been fulfilled? No. Christians need to be fed even more today the Word of God. The actions of most believers show they still do not fear God and do not know His Word. Even Jesus' final words to His disciples before ascending into heaven emphasize the importance of following God's commandments. In Matthew 28:20 we see, "Teach these new disciples to obey *all* the commands I have given you" (emphasis added). Which commands are these? How do we justify picking and choosing which commands to obey? We do not hesitate to recite, "Thou shalt not kill," but why not "Thou shalt not steal?"

I pray that by now you understand that tithing is not simply a matter of being Old Testament, New Testament, or Law of Moses, but that tithing is about knowing what God desires for us to do with the first 10 percent of our money that would be pleasing to Him.

Pay Yourself
(the second 10 percent)

According to Scripture, anyone who does not save money for the rainy day is a fool. Proverbs 21:20 says, "The wise have wealth and luxury, but fools spend whatever they get." Too many Christians do not have adequate savings upon which to draw when an unexpected obligation or bill comes along. Paying yourself second and building a solid financial foundation is the benchmark for great financial stewardship. No one can control things that might affect their daily life, such as sickness, car repairs, or home repairs, for example. But one can surely be prepared for these not to disrupt their regular routine if one has savings to cover these expenditures. Paying for the expenditures with credit cards is not good stewardship. Credit cards are simply ways to borrow against your future. While it may appear that credit cards have resolved the financial situation, the reality is that it is only a temporary fix—we simply trade one bill for another. The long-term result is that we are in more debt and with this continued pattern we find that we no longer control the debt, but that the debt controls us.

The Book of Proverbs is full of wonderful scripture that teaches valuable lessons about life. No scripture better than Proverbs 6:6–11 gives us the most valuable lesson about saving. This passage tells us to study the ways of the ants. The ants do not waste away their time, energy, and beautiful summer weather doing nothing. For the ants know that winter will come and they will be hungry. So they take the time when they can to put something aside for winter. We, as Christians, need to study the ways of the ant. Hopefully, the winters will not be so harsh that we need savings to fall back on. But if such a winter comes, it will be the wise Christian who is prepared and has saved. What we see far too often is that the unwise Christian has not saved and is in need. The unwise Christian has overspent and lives above his means. Then he gets behind in his bills and foreclosure is around the corner. The unwise Christian takes care of his desires and wants before taking care of his basic needs.

Then that unwise Christian wants the church or other religious organizations to bail them out of their financial mess. This is not biblical. The church does not exist to pay for poor stewardship! The church, according to the Bible, is supposed to feed and clothe the poor, not the fool (Prov. 21:20), and take care of the widows (1 Tim. 5:3).

Pay Your Obligations
(70 percent)

Romans 13:6–7 reminds us that we must not only pay our taxes, but that we must also pay whatever is owed by us to others. Being able to pay ourselves (savings after tithing) and to pay all our creditors on time, is really simply a matter of discipline and making good decisions. This is a good place to review Deuteronomy 14:22, which told us the purpose of tithing was to show that we feared God. If we take that scripture and connect it to Proverbs 1:28–31 we find that it is because Christians choose not to fear God that they are not able to gain the knowledge and wisdom that allow them to make good decisions. That scripture reads:

> When they cry for help, I will not answer. Though they anxiously search for me, they will not find me. For they hated knowledge and chose not to fear the LORD. They rejected my advice and paid no attention when I corrected them. Therefore, they must eat the bitter fruit of living their own way.

In order to make good decisions on how to spend the rest of your money, you must have good judgment. Proverbs 15:33 says, "Fear of the LORD teaches wisdom; humility precedes honor," while Proverbs

8:12 says, "I, Wisdom, live together with good judgment." Therefore, it is impossible for a Christian to have the kind of knowledge and wisdom that God wants them to have without having a fear of Him. We know that we truly fear God when we tithe, so that it is no longer lip service of love for God, but a deliberate intent in how we live and discipline ourselves with our finances in tithing.

It is amazing how many excuses Christians can come up with to justify not paying their bills or not paying them on time. No one forces any of us to create the bills in our life. With the exception of those individuals who have justifiable cases of a burden of bills—such as hospital bills resulting from inadequate insurance coverage, or a lay-off from a job because the company is moving or downsizing, but not because you got fired—most Christians created the financial situation they are in. The problem is they do not want to be honest with themselves and place the blame squarely where it belongs—with them. No one forced them to get a credit card and run it up with stuff as if their life depended on it. No one forced them to buy the expensive, gas-guzzler that they really could not afford. My father once told me, as I was about to purchase my first car, that "If you cannot afford the gas for the car, you cannot afford the car." No one forced them to purchase the three or four bedroom house in the nice neighborhood before they were really ready to pay for a mortgage and the insurance, taxes, and upkeep that came with it. No one forced them to eat out everyday. No one forced them to buy all the latest fashions, only to come to the first of the month and wonder where their money went!

It is time for the church to stop bailing these unwise Christians out of their situations—which are usually just temporary fixes that really do not address the problems of poor stewardship—and teach them about faithful, good stewardship. Instead, when someone who has exercised poor stewardship is about to lose their home, the church might be doing them a better favor by giving them enough money to pay a deposit and first month's rent on an apartment, and providing them a class on budgeting. What will they do next month when the mortgage is due again, if the non-payment resulted in the first place from a lack of poor decision-making? This situation is entirely different from someone in one of the exceptional cases described earlier. Surely the church is there to assist them however possible.

However, that is not the case in most financial crises. Many who come asking for assistance have huge cell phone bills, digital cable, expensive SUV's and cars. What they need is someone to show them good stewardship and decision-making—to first take care of their basic needs. First Timothy 5:8 (emphasis added) says:

But those who won't care for their relatives, especially those in their own household, have denied the true faith. Such people are *worse than unbelievers*.

Give to Others: Offerings (10 percent)

Offerings are gifts presented to God over and above the tithe. The entire Book of Deuteronomy refers to various offerings that can be given. It speaks of burnt offerings, sacrificial offerings, offerings to fulfill a vow, and many other offerings. There are many types of offerings because an offering represents your freewill giving to others for a purpose, or simply because God told you to bless someone with an offering. The offering is different from the tithe because the tithe is owed to God. Although you have the freewill choice in your life as to whether or not you will tithe, the tithe is expected by God to be given by you. (See Deuteronomy 14 and Malachi 3:8–11.) Offerings, however, are totally free of any obligation on your part to do so. Here is where many Christians willingly bless the church and other television ministries and organizations such as the United Way and Goodwill with offerings.

Let us explore offerings a little closer to our everyday life. An offering was used in the Bible to get God's attention when coming to the Temple and asking Him for forgiveness of sins or other poor discretional decisions. Offerings were also used for joyous occasions such as the birth of children (see Luke 2:23), appointed festivals, and even for peace. (See Leviticus 3; 23:8.) If offerings are extra and given in appreciation for something we want God to do, or for something God already has done in our lives, it is easy to make a comparison of offerings to modern day tips.

When we go to a restaurant, we receive our meals, and at the end of the meal decide how much to tip the waitress. If we have been pleased with the service, we will tip a minimum of 15 percent of the total cost of the meal. If we are comparing the cost of the meal along with the tip to our giving in the church, we could say that the cost of the meal is comparable to our tithes and the tip is our offering. The cost of the meal is owed. We ate the food, so we owe the bill. We believe the Word of God as it relates to tithing, so we owe the tithe. The tip, however, was given to show appreciation for something that was done on our behalf. If a waitress can earn a minimum of 15 percent for simply providing good service, how much more does God deserve for what He has done for us? We are quick to give God the praise for all He has done for us, but do we ever "tip" God? Once again, this goes back to the basic premise about Christians and their money and the quip from the preacher about Christians "hearing" from God. We will give God "praise," but we simply cannot give God our money. By tipping the waitress but not God, we are saying she is more worthy of a tip than our God. Not only do we as Christians tip waitresses, but we also tip bellhops at hotels, skycaps at airports, room service waiters at hotels, and valets who park our cars. The list can go on and on. We should be running to the altars in our local churches with our tips to God every time we think about the goodness of God and all He has done for us. A tip says "We appreciate you, God. Thank you for loving us."

CHAPTER 4

Getting Your Financial House in Order

What are firstfruits?

M ost Christians have been taught that firstfruits and tithes were the same. That is because it is taught that tithes are the first thing paid to God and therefore it becomes the firstfruit. While tithes are the first thing we should pay out of our income, it is not the same as firstfruits. Proverbs 3:9 makes a clear distinction by using the word *and*. Proverbs 3:9 says we should give to the Lord our "substance," which in different translations of the Bible appears as "wealth" or "income," and the first of our increases. There would be no need to repeat substance and increase if they were the same. Honoring the Lord with our substance is our tithe because substance is our income or wealth. The firstfruits of our increase honors God by giving Him the *first* of every increase we receive. In

Leviticus 27:26–32 we find a discussion about the firstfruits belonging to God. However, if we keep reading to verse 30, we find a discussion about the tenth—not the first tenth, but every tenth. In discussing the tithe, God did not ask for the *first* ten animals, because the discussion is about tithes and not firstfruits, but every tenth animal. The *first* of the animals have already been given to God in verse 26.

We have already explained that a tithe is 10 percent, not necessarily the *first*. We can go back and review the scriptures from Deuteronomy and Malachi. None of these scriptures that reference tithes say the tithe is the first. They say give a tithe or 10 percent. But a firstfruit is the *first*. Like the tithes, firstfruits are declared by God to be His, therefore it is not subject to our discretion the way offerings are. We read in Leviticus 27:26 (emphasis added):

> You may not dedicate a firstborn animal to the Lord, for the firstborn of your cattle, sheep, and goats already belong to him.

How is it that the *first* of everything already belongs to God? Turn back to Numbers 3:11–13 (emphasis added):

> And the Lord said to Moses, "Look, I have chosen the Levites from among the Israelites

> to serve as substitutes for all the firstborn sons
> of the people of Israel. The Levites belong to
> me, for all the firstborn males are mine. On
> the day I struck down all the firstborn sons
> of the Egyptians, I set apart for myself all the
> firstborn in Israel, both of people and of ani-
> mals. They are mine; I am the Lord."

If we remember the Exodus story, we know that
God had to send many plagues upon the Egyptian
people before they would allow the children of Israel
to leave Egypt. The final plague was the death of
every firstborn male child of the Egyptians including their livestock. (See Exodus 11:4–5.) Since God
saw in His grace to spare the lives of the firstborn
of the children of Israel, He simply asked that in
return the children of Israel would dedicate and give
back to God the first of all that they had. Therefore,
the firstfruits are the first of anything you receive. It
is your firstborn son, your first harvest of fruit, your
first harvest of apples, or your first paycheck or pay
increase. In simple terms, it is the *first* of anything.
It belongs to God. Does that sound crazy to you?
Read Leviticus 27 in its entirety and notice that it
talks about how to redeem for cash value a person,
animal, or thing that is suppose to be dedicated to
the Lord. Leviticus 27:26–33 goes on once again to
emphasize the difference between tithes, offerings,
and firstfruits. We can also refer to Deuteronomy

12:17 which references tithes, offerings, and first-fruits. They are not the same. Deuteronomy 12:17 (emphasis added) reads:

> But you may not eat your offerings in your hometown—neither the tithe of your grain and new wine and olive oil, nor the *firstborn* of your flocks and herds, nor any offering to fulfill a vow, nor your voluntary offerings, nor your sacred offerings.

Once again, the same messages are repeated by God:

Tithes, offerings, and firstfruits are not to be used by us at home, but belong to God. We can find many other passages that show that people in the Word of God honored the firstfruits principle and were blessed by it. In 2 Kings 4:42 (emphasis added), "One day a man from Baal-shalishah brought the man of God [Elisha] a sack of fresh grain and twenty loaves of barley bread made from the *first* grain of his harvest." Many people were fed from the first-fruit offering of bread with plenty left over. The message is this: an individual who believes in the firstfruits principle believes the firstfruit was given to God's representative. We also know the story of the woman with a son who was about to cook their last meal and die because they had only enough left to eat for one last meal. The prophet Elijah told the widow to go ahead and make the last meal, but to take what she had and make him a cake *first*, and then make one for herself and her son. (See 1 Kings 17:8–16.) Now most of us, if we are honest, will say the prophet Elijah ought to be ashamed of himself for taking what little the widow had when he already had so much. "How could he justify taking some of what little the widow had?" would be the question raised by many Christians. It is imperative, however, to say at this point that it would be the *immature* Christians who would only see the prophet taking away from the widow what little she already had. The mature Christian, however, will see God's principle at work, if only the widow would believe in God's principle of firstfruit.

With the principle of firstfruit, God is trying to teach us how to fish so we can stop asking for fish to eat. What does that mean? It means that the widow could have thought like other immature Christians and divided what she had between her and her sons. However, she did not see what immature Christians see. She believed and was blessed because she understood that it was not about what little she gave to the prophet. It was her faith in God's principle of firstfruits that enabled her to be blessed. She and her sons received a financial blessing by following the instructions of the prophet Elijah, after he received her firstfruit. The story did not end at verse 16, however. The widow's firstfruit blessing continued to operate in her life. Verses 17 through 24 go on to show how the widow was continually blessed later when her son became ill and died. Elijah came and prayed for her son asking God to give life back to the son. Her son was restored to life by God through Elijah's prayers.

We can also find in Nehemiah 10:32–39 the distinction between tithes, offerings, and firstfruits illustrated again. Here the people of God are promising to bring their *offerings* for the upkeep of the Temple (vv. 32–33), their *firstfruits* (verse 35), and their *tithes* to be given to the Levites (vv. 37–39).

Who were the Levites?

The Levites were individuals who were called by God to assist the priests in carrying out their duties in the Temple. They were not allowed in the inner courts, nor were they able to offer the sacrifices. Their jobs were as defined in Numbers 3:5–10:

> Then the Lord said to Moses, "Call forward the tribe of Levi, and present them to Aaron the priest to serve as his assistants. They will serve Aaron and the whole community, performing their sacred duties in and around the Tabernacle. They will also maintain all the furnishings of the sacred tent, serving in the Tabernacle on behalf of all the Israelites. Assign the Levites to Aaron and his sons. They have

been given from among all the people of Israel
to serve as their assistants. Appoint Aaron and
his sons to carry out the duties of the priesthood. But any unauthorized person who goes
too near the sanctuary must be put to death."

The Levites were chosen by God for the special
honor of assisting the priest because the Levites were
obedient to God. In Exodus 32:25–29 we read:

Moses saw that Aaron had let the people get com-
pletely out of control, much to the amusement
of their enemies. So he stood at the entrance to
the camp and shouted, "All of you who are on
the Lord's side, come here and join me." And
all the Levites gathered around him. Moses
told them, "This is what the Lord, the God of
Israel, says: Each of you, take your swords and
go back and forth from one end of the camp
to the other. Kill everyone—even your brothers, friends, and neighbors." The Levites obeyed
Moses' command, and about 3,000 people died
that day. Then Moses told the Levites, "Today
you have ordained yourselves for the service
of the Lord, for you obeyed him even though
it meant killing your own sons and brothers.
Today you have earned a blessing."

We can compare the Levites to today's church
leadership. We know that the New Testament

declares that we are all priests. We are a priesthood of believers. For when Jesus died, the veil of the Temple was rent (see Matthew 27:51) and we no longer needed a priest to be our representative before God. Jesus became our Representative before God. Who then are the modern-day Levites? The Levites were the assistants to the priest taking care of the temple. Therefore, the modern day Levites are those who work in the temple on behalf of our High Priest of today, Jesus Christ.

Most of us will agree that the pastor does work in the temple on behalf of Jesus Christ, and can therefore be called a modern-day Levite. If we agree on this, then we can go review a series of verses in Numbers 18 starting at verse 11:

> Verses 11–13: All the sacred offerings and special offerings presented to me when the Israelites lift them up before the altar also belong to you. I have given them to you and to your sons and daughters as your permanent share. Any member of your family who is ceremonially clean may eat of these offerings. I also give you the harvest gifts brought by the people as offerings to the Lord—the best of the olive oil, new wine, and grain. All the first crops of their land that the people present to the Lord belong to you.

Verse 14: Whatever is specially set apart for the Lord also belongs to you.

Verse 18: As for the tribe of Levi, your relative, I will pay them for their service in the Tabernacle with the *tithes* from the entire land of Israel. This is a permanent law among you. But the Levites will receive no inheritance of land among the Israelites, because I have given them the Israelites' tithes, which have been set apart as offerings to the Lord.

Verse 25: The Lord also told Moses, "Say this to the Levites; When you receive the tithes from the Israelites, give a tenth of the tithes you receive—a tithe of the tithe—to the Lord as a gift.

Verse 31: You Levites and your families may eat this food anywhere you wish, for it is your compensation for serving in the Tabernacle. You will not be considered guilty for accepting the Lords' tithes if you give the best portion to the priests.

There are many major points in this passage that need to be discussed. Having read the above scriptures, one would conclude that the tithes, offerings, and firstfruits should be brought to the church for the upkeep of the ministry and to compensate those who work in the Temple, known biblically as Levites. It has always been God's desire for those who work in the Temple to be compensated for their services. For in Nehemiah 12:44–47 we find (emphasis added):

> On that day men were appointed to be in charge of the storerooms for the gifts, the first part of the harvest, and the tithes. They were responsible to collect these from the fields as required by the law for the priests and Levites, for all the people of Judah *valued* the priests and Levites and their work. They performed the service of their God and the service of purification, as required by the laws of David and his son Solomon, and so did the singers and the gatekeepers. So now, in the days of Zerubbabel and of Nehemiah, the people brought a daily supply of food for the singers, the gatekeepers, and the Levites. The Levites, in turn, gave a portion of what they received to the priests, the descendants of Aaron.

Malachi 2:5–6 answers yet another reason *why* God desires that the tithes, offerings, and firstfruits be given to the Levites. We find these words:

> The purpose of my covenant with the Levites was to bring life and peace, and this is what I gave them. This called for reverence from

> them, and they greatly revered me and stood
> in awe of my name. They passed on to the
> people all the truth they received from me.
> They did not lie or cheat; they walked with
> me, living good and righteous lives, and they
> turned many from lives of sin.

God desired in His covenant with the Levites that they live good and righteous lives so that they can continue to teach God's Word and turn many sinners toward eternal salvation. Finally, it is God who determines who He desires to bless with what. God owns everything and has the right as the owner to distribute as He sees fit. It is not for us to question. We need to go back and read the entire Book of Job if we disagree with God's ability to give and take away.

Do not imply, however, from the previous discussion that *every time anyone does anything* for the Temple that they are to be compensated. This is far from the truth, for the Bible speaks of individuals giving of their time and talents to the work of the Lord. In 1 Chronicles 28:20–21 we find these words that support this point (emphasis added):

> Then David continued, "Be strong and cou-
> rageous, and do the work. Do not be afraid
> or discouraged by the size of the task, for the
> Lord God, my God, is with you. He will not

fail you or forsake you. He will see to it that all the work related to the Temple of the LORD is finished correctly. *The various divisions of priests and Levites will serve in the Temple of God. Others with skills of every kind will volunteer,* and the leaders and the entire nation are at your command.

We are specifically speaking now about those who are considered modern day Levites and are working full-time in the ministry of the Temple. The scriptures lifted from the Bible have made clear that God desires that the people value and honor those who labor in ministry. Full-time ministry, unfortunately, is also a misunderstood concept among many Christians. Some Christians believe that the only individual who should be paid is the pastor; and usually the pastor is not compensated well. Some Christians believe that the pastor should work a secular job to support himself. This is clearly not the intent of God. We find in the following scriptures support for the full-time ministry and financial support to those who are in ministry full-time.

In 2 Chronicles 31:4–5 we read:

In addition, he required the people in Jerusalem to bring the prescribed portion of their income to the priests and Levites, so they

> could devote themselves fully to the law of
> the Lord. The people responded immediately
> and generously with the *first* of their crops and
> grains, new wine, olive oil, honey, and all the
> produce of their fields. They brought a tithe of
> all they owned.

This scripture supports many concepts and principles laid out in this book. It supports: full-time
ministry, payment to those who work in full-time
ministry, firstfruits, tithes, and offerings. The passage is explicit that the priests and Levites were to
devote themselves full-time to the ministry of the
Lord's work. It does not say they need to work
somewhere else to supplement their income. If you
continue reading verses 5 through 20, you will find
that all the tithes, offerings, and firstfruits were so
plentiful that it was necessary for storerooms to be
built to house all the collections. Further in the
chapter, you also find that the tithes, offerings, and
firstfruits were then distributed to the priests and
Levites and all those who labored in the work of the
Temple.

There is also support for full-time ministry in Nehemiah 13:10–12:

> "I also discovered that the Levites had not
> been given what was due to them, so they and
> the singers who were to conduct the worship

> services had all returned to work their fields.
> I immediately confronted the leaders and
> demanded, "Why has the Temple of God been
> neglected?' Then I called all the Levites back
> again and restored them to their proper duties.
> And once more all the people of Judah began
> bringing their tithes of grain, new wine, and
> olive oil to the Temple storerooms."

Most Christians use the example of Paul as both
a preacher and tent maker as the illustration and
basis for dual career ministry. However, 1 Corinthians 9:3–14 reveals that this was not Paul's prefer-
ence nor his teaching:

> This is my answer to those who question my
> authority. Don't we have the right to live in
> your homes and share your meals? Don't
> we have the right to bring a Christian wife
> with us as the other apostles and the Lord's
> brothers do, and as Peter does? Or is it only
> Barnabas and I who have to work to support
> ourselves? What soldier has to pay his own
> expenses? What farmer plants a vineyard and
> doesn't have the right to eat some of its fruit?
> What shepherd cares for a flock of sheep and
> isn't allowed to drink some of the milk? Am I
> expressing merely a human opinion, or does
> the law say the same thing? For the law of
> Moses says, "You must not muzzle an ox to

keep it from eating as it treads out the grain." Was God thinking only about oxen when he said this? Wasn't he actually speaking to us? Yes, it was written for us, so that the one who plows and the one who threshes the grain might both expect a share of the harvest. Since we have planted spiritual seed among you, aren't we entitled to a harvest of physical food and drink? If you support others who preach to you, shouldn't we have an even greater right to be supported? But we have never used this right. We would rather put up with anything than be an obstacle to the Good News about Christ. Don't you realize that those who work in the temple get their meals from the offerings brought to the temple? And those who serve at the altar get a share of the sacrificial offerings. In the same way, the Lord ordered that those who preach the Good News should be supported by those who benefit from it.

One final point needs to be made with regard to full-time ministry, and/or dual career ministry concerning paying an individual who works in the Temple. Refer to Deuteronomy 18:6–8. When reading this scripture, one cannot help but see God's intent in compensating those who labor in ministry, regardless of their personal economic condition (emphasis added):

> Any Levite who so desires may come from any town in Israel, from wherever he is living to the place the Lord chooses. He may minister there in the name of the Lord his God, just like his fellow Levites who are serving the Lord there. He may eat his share of the sacrifices and offerings, *even if he has a private source of income.*

We just read in Numbers 18:31 that God says the Levites "will not be considered guilty for accepting the Lord's tithes, if [they] give the best portion to the priests." This simply means that the Levites can have plenty of other sources of income. It is not for other Christians to say "they do not need it" to justify their disobedience to God. The fact that Levites might be independently wealthy or have other sources of income does not take away from the responsibility of the people to obey God as it relates to tithes, offerings, and firstfruits. They still belong to the Levites. The Levites, in turn, now have a responsibility to do what God has directed them to do with the tithes, offerings, and firstfruits that they receive. They must give the best portion to the priests.

So what about the church mortgage? In most churches, a mortgage is the primary and largest debt. If tithes, offerings, and firstfruits were first intended for the workers, what then pays for the mortgage? In Exodus 35:1–33 and Exodus 36, when

God instructed Moses to build a Tabernacle for His name to be honored, He told Moses to tell the people (emphasis added):

> This is what the Lord has commanded. Everyone is invited to bring these *offerings* to the Lord: gold, silver, and bronze; blue, purple, and scarlet yarn; fine linen; goat hair for cloth; tanned ram skins and fine goatskin leather; acacia wood; olive oil for the lamps; spices for the anointing oil and the fragrant incense; onyx stones, and other stones to be set in the ephod and the chestpiece. Come all of you who are gifted craftsmen.
> —EXODUS 35:4–10, EMPHASIS ADDED

> So the whole community of Israel left Moses and returned to their tents. All whose hearts were stirred and whose spirits were moved came and brought their sacred offerings to the LORD. They brought all the materials needed for the Tabernacle, for the performance of its rituals, and for the sacred garments. Both men and women came, all whose hearts were willing.
> —EXODUS 35:20–22

> So the people of Israel—every man and woman who was eager to help in the work the LORD had given them through Moses—

85

brought their gifts and gave them freely to the LORD.

—Exodus 35:29

Moses gave them the materials donated by the people of Israel as sacred offerings for the completion of the sanctuary. But the people continued to bring additional gifts each morning. Finally the craftsmen who were working on the sanctuary left their work. They went to Moses and reported, "The people have given more than enough materials to complete the job the LORD has commanded us to do!" So Moses gave the command, and this message was sent throughout the camp: "Men and women, don't prepare any more gifts for the sanctuary. We have enough!" So the people stopped bringing their sacred offerings. Their contributions were more than enough to complete the whole project.

—Exodus 36:3–7

So how does the Bible provide for the building of a church? Ask the people of God to give their gifts—gifts of money, time, talents, and skills. Ask the people of God to continue to give daily until there are enough materials on hand to complete the *whole* project. Those who have a willingness and desire in their hearts to give will give.

There is no mention, once again, of tithes, offerings, and firstfruits being used to build the sanctuary. Gifts from the people built the tabernacle. Unfortunately, many churches lack the membership of individuals who have lived the financial principles of the Bible for a period long enough to be able to bring such gifts for the building of any church project. If the people of God would begin to educate their children at an early age about financial stewardship and how they should handle their money, there would never be lack in the church. Every Christian would be able to give to the church and still not lack in their personal lives.

Conclusion

So, how much is too much for a Christian to keep? If we follow the biblical guidelines presented and use the percentages outlined, there is no dollar amount and there will always be those who can and should live extremely well. For example, one individual might earn a million dollars a year and will give away 10 percent or even 20 percent of their earnings and still live better than someone who makes, say, one hundred thousand dollars a year. Christians need to stop judging an individual on what they have, instead of what one gives away! It is usually the person who does not give even the commanded 10 percent who is complaining about the person who gave more than 20 percent of their income away. If a person is blessed by God to have a profession that pays well, is that person supposed to give 50 or 60 percent of their income away to please those who believe individuals should not live in a certain lifestyle? What is an acceptable lifestyle for Christians? How many square feet should their house be? Should all Christians live in a house no larger than two thousand square feet? What is the maximum amount of money a Christian should spend on their car? Should all Christians be limited to two cars that cost less than twenty thousand dollars each? What is the maximum amount of money a Christian should have in the bank? Is ten thousand dollars in the bank too much for a Christian to have? How about one hundred thousand dollars? Who decides all that?

Contrary to popular opinion, the Bible does not tell Christians nor those who preach the gospel to take a vow of poverty. Enough scriptures have been raised within the context of this book to prove that God's original intent for all mankind is to live a lifestyle other than that which is lifted in the media as appropriate for those of the faith. The Bible is clear that there will be some who will take a vow of sacrifice for the faith, such as those who will never marry, or will never drink alcoholic beverages, and even poverty. However, never from Genesis to Revelation does the Bible say that Christians or anyone of the faith must take a vow of poverty.

It is ridiculous to even begin to fathom someone setting such standards for anybody, let alone Christians. There are too many variables. There can be two Christians that make the same amount of money, yet live two totally different lifestyles from the outside. One can decide to have an expensive house and car and eat beans and franks for dinner and make all their clothes. Another can choose to dine out for dinner each night and have antiques throughout their modest home, yet drive an economical car. They each give their 10 percent. Who decides which Christian is living the way they should be living? Based on common standards, one might think the one living in the big house and driving a luxury car is not being a good steward. How does one come to that conclusion when both are giving the same amount away?

Jesus was clear to us when He said that He did not judge a man by outside appearance, but by their heart and their motives. Jesus went on to say that, unfortunately, we see sometimes too often with only our eyes. A well-known evangelist once said that his goal was to live on 10 percent of his income and to give away 90 percent. Yet upon closer examination, 10 percent of millions of dollars in income would provide a lifestyle that many still would frown upon for an individual in ministry!

So, now you see why God had to spend so much time in the Bible speaking about money and what our attitude about money should be. Right now we are in the midst of what one day will simply be yet another frontier story with the reader having the benefit of living in the future and the hindsight to put money and theology into a healthy perspective that we seem unable to today. I guess the old saw, "We can't see the forest for the trees," might be appropriate at this point in time.

But what will history record as your role in shaping how the frontier story ends? Will you continue to carry on the debate as to whether Jesus was financially rich or financially poor to justify how one should live, without really being able for yourself to biblically support either case? Will you continue to criticize the lifestyle of those in ministry, or any Christian who lives according to Deuteronomy 8? Will you continue to live above your financial means expecting others to bail you out of financial crises, instead of living within the guidelines established by God for you? Or will history record that you were one who heard the voice of God speak to you about money and the Bible? Will history state that you finally got on the road of God's financial plan for your life, understanding that while enjoying the fruits of your labor is surely God's desire, His ultimate desire is that you use your finances to further the gospel, empower the church, and bless others who are less fortunate? Or, in other words, were you obedient to God and did with your wealth what He commands you to do?

Biblical Financial Spending Plan

Use the chart starting on page 95 to start your journey to God's plan for your financial freedom. The chart is a guide to assist you in developing a spending plan that will enable you to have the financial freedom that God desires for you and your household. In using the chart, make sure you do the following:

Step One: List all your income, but *do not* list income that is not consistent, such as overtime or a temporary job. Your spending should be based on income that you can count on and that you will consistently receive.

Step Two: List only those expenses that are needed for your *basic needs.* This may be difficult for those of you who are already in a lot of debt with expensive cars and mortgages that you cannot afford. If this is the case, you may want to consider downsizing those items to have an affordable and achievable spending plan.

If you do not have this debt, take this opportunity to lay a good, solid foundation toward your financial future. Your goal should be to have extra money left over after taking care of your basic needs. It is only after you have taken care of your basic needs that you are ready to consider purchasing your wants and desires.

The ultimate goal is to plan for contingencies—those unexpected bills without having to ask the church, your family, or friends for financial assistance.

You are not ready to indulge in wants and desires until you have saved at least three to six months of your basic living expenses in your savings account. This is not an investment account nor your retirement account, but a basic low interest savings account from which you can retrieve money anytime you need to. Once you have saved this amount of money, you will be able to take care of unexpected bills without creating new bills. You will also be able to take care of unexpected income declines without losing your car or house and until you have time to find another job. Remember, a disaster created by somebody else should not create a disaster in your life!

Step Three: Add up all your basic needs and subtract this amount from your income. This amount becomes the basis of how much you should have in your savings account, which is three to six times this amount. You should save three times this amount if your income is less than fifty thousand dollars. If your income is more than fifty thousand dollars per year, then you need to save at least six times your basic expenses. This is because statistics say that it takes a person who makes more than fifty thousand dollars a year at least six months to find a job paying that amount of money. Remember, your goal is not to lose everything simply because you might get laid off. Be prepared. Go back and study the ways of the ants in Proverbs.

If there is income left over and after you have your savings intact, then you are ready to indulge—a little—and increase your standard of living. This is where you are now ready to add extra luxuries in life to your spending plan. Now you can upgrade that basic car to a more moderate car, or start looking to move out of the apartment into a condo, or townhouse, or a starter home.

Do not forget to keep saving—you never stop saving, even after your reach your three-to-six-month goal. Your increased savings over and above this amount is where you can begin to start investing in mutual funds or stocks for your added retirement planning and college funds for your children.

Step Four: After you have completed steps one

through three and still have extra money left, you are *really* ready to enjoy life. By now you should have substantial savings, be well on your way to retirement (at whatever age you may have set), pay your bills on time, and have excellent credit. If this is not the case, you need to go back, start again, and revisit what you are calling basic expenses.

If you have been disciplined enough to reach this point, you know that you can truly have your desires without fear of your ability to pay the expenses. Go ahead and upgrade your home, your car, or take that dream vacation.

BIBLICAL FINANCIAL SPENDING PLAN

	Income			
	Income Sources	You	Spouse	Monthly Total
	Wages/Pension (net)			
	Interest/Dividends			
	Other			
Line 1	Income Total			

BIBLICAL FINANCIAL SPENDING PLAN

	Expenses (Basic Needs)			
	Description	Amount		
	Tithes			
	Savings			
	Mortgage/Rent			
	Child Care			
	Clothing			
	Groceries			
	Electricity			
	Gas/home			
	Oil			
	Water/sewage			
	Telephone			
	Car Payment			
	Gas/car			
	Auto Insurance			
	Life Insurance			
	Medical Insurance			
	Dental Insurance			
	Vision Insurance			
	Medical Co-pay			
	Prescriptions			
	Medicines (Others)			
Line 2	Total Expenses			
Line 3	Net Income Available Wants (line 1 minus line 2)			1

BIBLICAL FINANCIAL SPENDING PLAN

	Expenses (Wants)			
	Description	Amount		
	Cable/Satellite TV			
	Pet/Vet			
	Home Security			
	Lawn Service			
	Housecleaning Service			
	Home Improvement			
	Garden Supplies			
	Cellular Telephone			
	Internet Provider			
	Dry Cleaning			
	Salon/Barber			
	Mag/News/Books			
	Dining Out			
	Theater/Night Club			
	Movies/Concerts			
	Music (CDs, etc.)			
	Rentals: Videos/DVD			
	Vacation			
	Gifts: Special Occa.			
Line 4	Wants Totals			
Line 5	Net Income Available Desires (line 3 minus line 4)			2

BIBLICAL FINANCIAL SPENDING PLAN

	Expenses (Desires)			
	Description	Amount		
	Luxury Car			
	Charitable Giving			
	Social Club Dues			
	Health Club/Gym Fees			
	Larger Home Mortgage			
	Team Dues			
	Car Wash/Detailing			
	Pet Care (kennel, etc.)			
Line 6	Desire Totals			
Line 7	Net Income Remaining (line 5 minus line 6)			3

1	Line 1 minus line 2	=	Net Income Available for WANTS
2	Line 3 minus line 4	=	Net Income Available for DESIRES
3	Line 5 minus line 6	=	Net Income Remaining

Epilogue

For those who have read the preceding pages, much has been shared that is new and revelatory for you. Our prayer is that you reread, meditate, and pray on what you have read. God, in His infinite wisdom, will guide you in your understanding of that which has been shared.

As articulated in the Preface and Introduction, it has not been my desire in this book to contradict any previous teachings or denominational traditions. The desire and motivation for this book has truly been an inspiration from God to further enlighten the Christian community on His teachings on prosperity doctrine and finance.

I pray God will bless the efforts that went into publishing this book, and that the increase will go to Him. To God be the glory for that which He has done. Amen.

Notes

Preface

1. *The New Believer's Bible*, New Living Translation (Wheaton, IL: Tyndale House Publishers, Inc., 1996), A31.

Chapter 2:
God's Original Plan for Our Financial Freedom

1. *Merriam-Webster's Collegiate Dictionary, 11th Edition* (Springfield, MA: Merriam-Webster, 2003).

Chapter 3:
Managing Our Money God's Way

1. *Merriam-Webster's Collegiate Dictionary, 11th Edition* (Springfield, MA: Merriam-Webster, 2003).

About the Author

Valerie K. Brown is a native of Chesapeake, Virginia. She readily serves beside her husband, the Rev. Dr. Kim Walter Brown, Senior Pastor of Mount Lebanon Missionary Baptist Church, also in Chesapeake. She serves as the Executive Pastor. Together they are the proud parents of two children, James and Kimberly.

Elder Brown has an earned doctorate degree in Business Management from the Weatherhead School of Management at Case Western Reserve University in Cleveland, Ohio. She received her CPA certification in 1980 in Virginia. She has previously taught Church Administration, Finance, and Leadership in the Master of Divinity Program at the Samuel D. Proctor School of Theology at Virginia Union University in Richmond, Virginia.

Other Books by This Author

I n *What's in a Title?* Dr. Valerie K. Brown dispels the myths about the usage of titles in the modern-day church. The New Testament specifically outlines roles and functions for leaders, which includes titles. But, the purpose and need for these ministry gifts go beyond denominational lines or personal exaltation. Dr. Brown will take you beyond the proverbial "fluff" to uncover the true purpose for labeling church leaders and discern the authentic from the counterfeit.